GLASS JEWELLERY

GLASS JEWELLERY

Yvonne Coffey

A & C Black • London

First published in Great Britain in 2009
A & C Black Publishers Limited
36 Soho Square
London W1D 3QY
www.acblack.com

ISBN: 978-07136-7940-3

CIP Catalogue records for this book are available from the British Library and the U.S. Library of Congress.

Typeset in 10.5 on 13pt Minion

Book design by Jo Tapper
Cover design by Sutchinda Rangsi Thompson
Commissioning Editor: Susan James
Managing Editor: Sophie Page

Frontispiece: Necklace by Rebecca Cheeseman

WKT: Printed in China by WKT Company Ltd

A & C Black uses paper produced with elemental chlorine-free pulp, harvested from managed sustainable forests.

CAUTION: Working with glass and operating kilns, tools and machinery are dangerous activities. Please use adequate safeguards when attempting any of the activities described in this book because you assume all associated risks. The publishers cannot be held responsible in the case of any accident or injury resulting from any procedure or instruction included here.

Contents

ACKNOWLEDGEMENTS

I have had many wonderful people help me with this book and I owe them all many thanks for their guidance and support.

Firstly, I'd like to thank Susan James at A&C Black for giving me the chance to write this book, and for all her help and advice during the writing process. I'd also like to thank Sophie Page and the rest of the staff at A&C Black for their help.

I'd especially like to thank Yvonne Kulagowski as she has supported me and my work throughout my career and inspired me to write this book. Special thanks also to all the artists whose work features in this book. Thanks to Debbi Collins, Emi Fujita, Yoko Kuramoto, Amanda Simmons and Angela Thwaites for sparing the time and effort to help me with this endeavor and providing me with an insight into their working methods. This book could not have been finished without the advice and technical help of Pearsons Glass, Creative Glass, Bullseye Glass, Bohle and Storm Jewellery.

Also special thanks to Andrew Pritchard for his wonderful photographs plus his invaluable advice on photography and to Takako Tucker for working patiently with me on the diagrams.

I'd like to pay special tribute and thanks to my mum and my partner, Jeff, for their patience, and support and for giving me the time and space needed to complete this work. And also to my little boy Bryn, to whom I dedicate this book.

Introduction

I have worked with glass, and glass jewellery, for 20 years, exhibiting, teaching and developing courses. I embarked upon this book because of my passion for the subject and my wish to share my experience with others. Glass jewellery has always intrigued me. I am fascinated by the way people put glass on their bodies to adorn them and by the way this has happened down the centuries. The human need for adornment has never changed.

Why kiln-formed glass jewellery? Well, I like the processes involved in kiln-forming. They allow for a variety of qualities. There is a dynamic involved in the movement of what goes on in the kiln. Also, the decision-making is varied, and decisions can be made, and different directions taken, at several different stages.

Despite its pivotal place in history, glass remains a very contemporary material. Its own history has been continually reinvented, the experimentation and innovation with glass as a form of jewellery being constant down the ages. In this book I hope to demonstrate these many, and varied, approaches to making glass jewellery with the help of the artists who have graciously agreed to contribute.

Necklace by Yvonne Coffey. Photograph by Joel Degen.

1. A Brief History of Glass and Glass Jewellery

There is much dispute surrounding the origins of glass. It is thought that the earliest glass was created when rocks melted in extreme temperatures due either to volcanic eruptions, lightning strikes or the impact of meteorites. Many scientists believe that the earliest use of glass was by Stone Age humans, who used cutting tools made from strong forms of glass such as obsidian. More certain is the fact that glass is one of the earliest manmade materials, its use dating back as far as 3500 BC.

Glass has always been adaptable to many functions, but one of its most significant early uses was for adornment. Non-transparent glass beads from the 4th millennium BC have been found in Egypt and what used to be Eastern Mesopotamia. These beads were traded across the coasts of the Mediterranean by Phoenician merchants and sailors.

The capacity of glass to resemble expensive gemstones gave it a widespread appeal, and aesthetically glass jewellery could be as fashionable as its gemstone counterparts.

Ancient jewellery was frequently linked with religion, designed either to praise a revered deity or protect against a feared one. In many societies, figurative pendants or necklaces, representing the gods of a particular culture, were often cast in glass.

Ancient glassworkers often worked metals, particularly gold, into their designs, while glass rings were also commonplace in ancient Egypt and Greece.

By the 9th century BC glassmaking was becoming more prevalent and, from two centuries later, instructions on how to make glass can be found in tablets that were kept in the library of the Assyrian king,

Ashurbanipal, who reigned from 669 to 626 BC. Some of these tablets are now housed in the British Museum in London.

The global spread of glass came in the 4th and 3rd centuries BC. It was during this period that glassmaking is thought to have started in Italy. The Roman Empire, with its conquests and the subsequent network of trading relations, did much to disseminate glassmaking technology, so that glass production and trade duly flourished.

Glass jewellery was everywhere in Roman society. It was not just a favourite of female Roman nobility. Under the Romans, Germany and the Rhineland became a centre for glassmaking and for glass jewellery, which began to appear throughout Europe and was even found as far away as China. However, as with many technical advances achieved during this period, the decline of the Roman Empire in the 4th and 5th centuries AD saw the craft of glassmaking wane in Europe.

Nevertheless, as the Continent gradually recovered from that cultural collapse, so did the arts the Romans had introduced. One of the first signs of glass jewellery in Europe, outside Roman influence, dates from 8th-century Bohemia, now part of the Czech Republic. Glass furnaces were used to produce glass costume jewellery, which was tremendously popular in that region.

This was a rare occurrence, though. Elsewhere in Europe, the revival of glass was limited, in the main focusing on the development of stained-glass windows for cathedrals and monasteries in the 11th and 12th centuries AD. However, Europe was later to be responsible for one of the most important periods in glassmaking and glass jewellery-making.

Venice became the glassmaking centre of the Western world. Until the end of the 13th century, historians say most glassmaking in Venice took place in the city itself. However, frequent fires caused by the furnaces led the city authorities to order the transfer of glassmaking to the island of Murano. By the end of the 16th century, almost half of the island's inhabitants were involved in the glassmaking industry. Glass from Venice and Bohemia proved highly popular for many centuries.

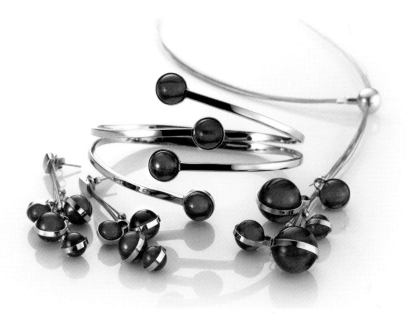

Red Beril Group by STORM. Crystal glass glued into silver

By the late 17th century, George Ravenscroft had patented lead glass. This brought an improvement in glass-cutting for jewellery. Before the 18th century, jewellery had been limited to the aristocratic ladies of the court. But now the wearing of glass jewellery became more widespread, and became affordable for a wider section of the public.

By the 19th century, glass jewellery had taken a foothold in America and especially in France. Today glass continues to be a popular medium through which artists can express themselves and their concepts in the form of jewellery. These pieces adorn millions of people worldwide.

2. *What Glass to Use*

In this chapter, I shall examine which glass is best to use. Before embarking on any project, it is worth discussing the properties of glass and how these can influence the choice of material you are going to work with. As you develop your knowledge of glass, you will be able to anticipate this process and forge a clearer understanding of how to get the best from your work. To help you do this, it is best to keep comprehensive records. The more you work with glass, the more your understanding of this most intriguing of materials will improve.

The qualities you will need to consider for any given project are:

- Compatibility
- Types and forms of glass
- Hard and soft glass
- Colour changes (striking)
- Devitrification.

I will cover these areas individually, but in any case you will become more familiar with the terminology as you read through each chapter.

COMPATIBILITY

Like most materials, when glass is heated it expands, and when it cools it contracts. The amount by which a particular glass expands and contracts can be measured and quantified. This is expressed as the linear 'Coefficient of Expansion' (CoE) and is given a number for reference. Different makes of glass will vary in their expansion rates, because of the various ingredients manufacturers use in their recipes. For example, Bullseye is 90, while Spectrum is 96.

When two pieces of glass of different makes are melted together using heat, they become one coherent mass. If these two pieces expand at different rates once they have fused and cooling begins, strains could appear which may result in cracking and instability known as incompatibility. However, the coefficient of expansion is only a rough guide as to how well two glasses will fit. The viscosity of the glass (how much the glass flows) also plays a role and needs to be considered. For example, two makes of glass can have the same CoE, but one may be much softer and more fluid while the other may be harder and more rigid. On cooling, the more rigid glass will force the softer one to manoeuvre around it, thus causing stress. The CoE number is only calculated up to 300°C (572°F), and the expansion rate of glass alters at various temperatures throughout the firing cycle, so the CoE should only be used as a starting point. The various strains set up by the expansion of the glass and its viscosity can work together to make glass pieces with differing CoE numbers work together once fired. If the tensions set up by the differing expansion rates are balanced by the tensions set up by the differing viscosities, the glass will fire successfully. However, the glass will still need to be fully annealed (see Chapter 10).

An incompatibility crack is very distinctive, and will often appear as a visible separation between the two different glasses. However, not all incompatible glass will show a visible crack, and incompatibility makes the glass unstable and can lead to cracking or shattering later on. Thus it is important to know whether such stress is present, and to check for it using a stressometer or polarised filters.

A test strip is a good way of testing for compatibility along with viscosity, susceptibility to devitrification, and changes in colour (striking) due to

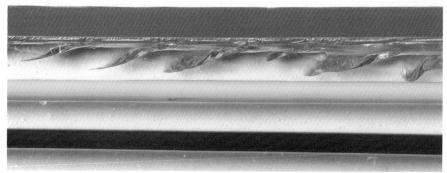

Stringers have been fused on to sheet. The two are not compatible. Cracks can be seen where the stringers have melted. Photograph by Andrew Pritchard

Test strip using sheet glass note how the light blue glass (third from the right) has devitrified. Photograph by Andrew Pritchard

the firing. It is a very good starting point from which to begin to unravel all the variables in kiln-formed glass.

Making a test strip

- Cut a base strip 3 x 25 cm (1.2 x 10 in.). The length can vary depending on how many pieces of glass are being tested.
- Cut a 2 cm (0.8 in.) piece off the end of the strip. Cut this into a square and place it onto the original base strip. This will act as your control. If there is a problem with the firing and annealing does not take place cracks may appear. It could be hard to spot that these are the result of poor annealing. If the cracks appear on the control square it could alert you to potential annealing problems, as glass from the same sheet is compatible with itself.
- Once the control is in place, cut out squares from the pieces of glass to be tested. Ensure they are all 2 x 2 cm (0.8 x 0.8 in.). Making them consistent reduces the variables and gives regular information with which to assess the results.
- Place the squares 1.5 cm (0.6 in.) apart along the base strip. It is very important the squares do not touch, as this could confuse results. The test is to show which glass is compatible with the base strip, but if the squares are allowed to touch, they may crack if they are not compatible

with each other. It would then be difficult to distinguish these cracks from any problems that occur through contact with the base glass.
• Fire the strip to a full fuse and anneal.

Now the strip is fired. The next step is visually to check the control square for any cracks. If there are any, then there may have been a problem with the firing (See chapter 10 for firing information). If all is well with the firing, look at the remaining squares. If there are any obvious cracks running between the base strip and the test square, these are incompatibility cracks. The base and the square have fused together at top temperature, but because they shrink at different rates relating to their different CoEs or viscosities they may have sheared apart on cooling to the solid state. These are the easy ones to spot. The test strip now needs to be viewed through a stressometer or polarising filters.

It is possible to test for incompatibility without using a kiln by doing a thread test. This is quick and very useful when an immediate answer is required, but it does not provide the fullest information as to how the glass behaves when fired.

First, you should **always wear goggles** when heating glass in a flame. Prepare two strips, or rods, of the glass to be tested and ensure they are of equal thickness and dimension. Place these in a flame with sufficient

Making a test strip using frit
Test strip for frit and powder. The frit must be piled up into compartments constructed of sheet glass on a base of sheet glass. This makes the frit thick enough to potentially expose any stress.
Photograph by Andrew Pritchard

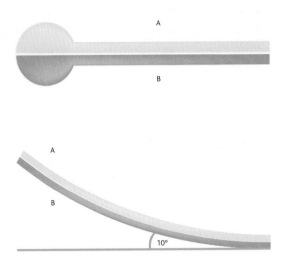

Thread test
The glass needs to be melted to a ball, but the two glasses must not mingle, or the test will not be accurate. When the glass is pulled the angle of curve must not exceed 10 degrees. Diagram by Takako Tucker

heat to melt the ends of the glass. Next allow each glass strip to form a coherent blob at the end. The molten ends should fuse, but should not mix and become twisted.

When carrying out this test, you should aim to have A and B strips of equal thickness. This should give you the most accurate results.

While the blob of glass is still molten, grab the rounded end with a pair of tweezers and pull the glass out in a straight line to obtain a fine thread. Once this has been achieved, allow the thread to cool, separate it from the two ends, and place it next to a straight edge. It should now be possible to observe how straight, or curved, the glass thread is. By doing this, it is easier to judge the results: the more the curve, the greater the incompatibility (the less compatible the glass pieces). The glass thread curves because one side (A) is shrinking more than the other (B). If the amount of expansion and contraction is too great, the joined glass will crack through being unstable. The curve should not exceed 10 degrees over a length of 30 cm (12 in.) if the glass is going to be viable.

In summary, the greater the curve in the glass, the greater the difference in shrinkage, and thus the greater the incompatibility of the two pieces of glass. This thread test can be a very useful and quick method of calculating the degree of compatibility.

TYPES AND FORMS OF GLASS

It is worth being aware of the range of glass available, as the type and quality of material you choose to work with will affect the final piece. Glass comes in a wide range of forms: sheet, ingot, cullet, frit, stringers,

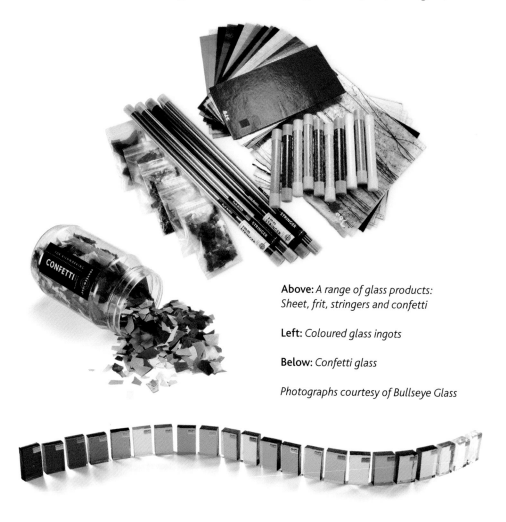

Above: *A range of glass products: Sheet, frit, stringers and confetti*

Left: *Coloured glass ingots*

Below: *Confetti glass*

Photographs courtesy of Bullseye Glass

powder, confetti, recycled bottles, beads, marbles, slabs, ballotini, shards, rods and millefiori. All these types of glass can come in a wide range of colours, transparencies and hardnesses, all qualities you need to consider. Below are descriptions of the different types of glass available. Colour and transparency are a matter of personal aesthetic, but the hardness, or

Ballotini Small round glass balls used either for sandblasting or in chemical filtration. They come in a range of glass types; some are soda lime and can be compatible with window-glass sheet.

Confetti Very thin fragile wisps of glass created by blowing fine large bubbles, cooling and then bursting to create confetti; very effective when layered over clear sheet.

Cullet Irregular chunks for casting.

Frit Anything from rock-salt size to fine granules.

Ingot Large pieces for casting.

Pattern bars or Millefiori These can be made, or purchased, and have a design running all the way through like seaside rock. They can be cut and used in small slices.

Powder Medium to fine powder.

Recycled bottle, beads or Marbles All these types of glass are readily available. Don't underestimate their usefulness, but bear in mind the issue of incompatibility. Bottles from the same manufacturer stand a good chance of being compatible, but marbles and beads can, because of their annealing and manufacture, even from the same batch and day, be incompatible. So use with caution. It only takes one incompatible marble in a piece to cause a crack. So it is always a gamble if they are used for larger-scale work.

Rods Larger, straighter bars of glass.

Shards Sharp splinters of glass.

Sheet Either floated onto molten tin, rolled to create a texture or blown into tubes.

Slabs Thick cast sheet in a range of colours, useful for casting or directly cold working.

Stringers Thin threads of glass available in a range of colours; also known as spaghetti glass due to its shape.

softness, of glass is a more practical choice, determined by how easily it will melt in the kiln, its viscosity. This is something that will show up in a test-strip firing.

HARD AND SOFT GLASS

Glass can vary from hard to soft, and some of this will be apparent from the test strip. 'Hard' doesn't necessarily refer to the durability or resistance to grinding of a piece of glass, but gives an indication of its viscosity and the level of heat required to melt it. Hard glass tends to need greater heat to achieve a successful melt or fuse; soft glass requires a lower heat to reach the same results.

COLOUR CHANGES (STRIKING)

Some glass has a predisposition to change colour during a firing. This is known as 'striking'. The reds and ruby colours are the most vulnerable, although some colours will only develop to their full vibrancy once fired.

DEVITRIFICATION

As it has no crystal structure, glass is transparent. Its lack of crystal structure is due to the particular balance of ingredients and its viscosity. The viscosity delays the development of crystals on cooling. Devitrification can happen when crystals are able to establish themselves due to an imbalance of ingredients. So why and how does this imbalance happen? By understanding the mechanisms involved it will be possible to adjust firings, select appropriate glass, or even encourage devitrification for creative use. Although it can be a thorn in the side for the kiln worker, devitrification has been used by some makers to great effect. But understanding and control is the key.

An imbalance in the chemical composition of the glass may occur when the glass is subjected to high temperatures in the kiln over a period of time. When the glass goes from being a solid to being a liquid, certain ingredients are able to evaporate, and this will continue as long as the glass is being fired above its softening point. The crystal growth will only occur on the surface, which is why devitrification is more of an issue for static fusing and slumping rather than mobile casting. Different types of glass will have a greater or lesser tendency to devitrify. This is something which can be assessed while doing test strips for compatibility. Bearing in mind the inherent tendency of the glass to devitrify, other factors can contribute to crystals forming. I have outlined areas to check, and the solutions, below.

Problem: Contamination on the surface of the piece.
Solution: Clean all glass thoroughly before stacking and firing.

Problem: Contamination in the kiln.
Solution: Hoover (vacuum) the kiln prior to loading.

Problem: Holding the kiln at a high temperature for too long, allowing more time for unwanted crystal formation.
Solution: Keep firing for as short a time as possible above the annealing point, and be in attendance to crash-cool (see firing curves and schedules).

Problem: Other materials in the kiln burning off during the firing, e.g. organic inclusions, wax, binders, metals, fabrics, tape, enamels, china clay, etc.
Solution: Always vent the kiln and keep additional materials to a minimum where possible.

3. The Cutting and Preparation of Glass

We've dealt with the raw material and all the differences in size, shape and colour of glass. This chapter will look at how to cut, shape and prepare glass for use.

When discussing the cutting of glass, I will refer to float glass. This is also known as, or referred to as, window or soda glass. Later, I will run through the most commonly encountered problems when cutting and preparing glass, and I will also outline various troubleshooting techniques. The aim of this is to improve the recognition and understanding of any problems encountered.

When you are learning to cut glass, a great place to start practising is on float, the common sheet glass found in most windows. It is made to very consistent standards of thickness and hardness, and contains no imperfections. This type of glass is also readily available and relatively cheap – it may even be free if you can persuade your local double-glazing firm to let you raid their skip. The low costs involved can be useful in the early stages of the making process, as this generally limits the stress of worrying about the mounting costs of each project. When practising, it is crucial to stay relaxed and focused, and not to fret about calculating the cost of each score.

TOOLS FOR CUTTING SHEET GLASS

- A good clear working surface covered with carpet, felt or thick newspaper
- Safety glasses
- Apron
- Glasscutter
- Glass-cutting oil
- Cut spreaders
- Grozing pliers
- Square edge
- Marker pen
- Dustpan and brush

Tools for cutting glass. From left: grozing pliers, pistol-grip oil-filled glass cutter, ball-end glass cutter, grip oil cutter, oil-filled glass cutter. Photograph provided by Creative Glass

CUTTING GLASS SUCCESSFULLY

Ensure you have a flat clear working surface at just below waist height. Make sure it is covered with carpet, felt or a wad of newspaper. This prevents the glass from being scratched and provides a cushion for support. Make sure, too, that you clean the glass thoroughly, as grease and dust will interfere with the wheel of the glasscutter on the surface of the glass.

It is also important to have enough room in which to work. You will need to be able to move your whole arm and body freely to make strong fluid scores with your cutter.

Remember that glass cuts better at room temperature. So allow time for the glass to warm up before cutting, especially if it has been stored in a cold place.

Always break glass immediately after scoring. This prevents the glass 'healing', something that is especially important to avoid when using thicker glass. Make the cut in one continuous movement. It is not possible to restart a cut halfway across the glass, so don't stop once you've started cutting. You only have one chance. Don't be tempted to go over a score line again. This just crushes the glass and damages the wheel on the cutter. It's best to just move on and make a new cut.

Making a straight cut

A good thickness of glass to start learning to cut on is 2 to 4mm. The thicker the glass is, the harder it is to cut and make a good clean break.

Preparing your working area

When preparing a work area, it is best to choose a flat, even surface with no joins or gaps. The workspace should be one at which you can stand comfortably. This is often just below waist height. But the best judge of what is, or is not, comfortable is yourself. The more cutting you do, the more you will know what makes you feel comfortable. Always clean the surface after use to remove accumulated shards of glass created by the

---

Health and safety

- Always wear eye protection. Even if you wear glasses, it is essential to use protective goggles. In the event of an accident, they can be replaced, but you only have one pair of eyes.
- Protective clothing is also important. Wear an apron, or an extra layer of clothing. Do not bare your midriff. Your stomach is vulnerable with sheet glass at table height. The same consideration needs to be given to your wrists – be careful not to expose them and always get help when you're carrying a large sheet. When moving glass ensure you have a clear route with enough room. Always carry glass vertically. If it is a large piece, do not attempt it on your own. Always get help.
- Newly cut edges are very sharp, so be careful.
- Never leave glass sheet balanced half on and half off the work surface.
- Always concentrate on what you are doing. Don't try to cut glass when you are distracted.
- Always store glass vertically in a wooden rack and make sure there are no edges sticking out.
- Never lean on glass, or place any tools on or under it.

---

cutting process. Also, if you are going to be doing regular cutting, it would be wise to cover your surface with a thick layer of underlay and secure it permanently with tacks on the underside.

Alternatively, if space is at a premium, the work surface can be covered with several layers of newspaper to create a similar cushioned surface. Start with a generous pile of newspaper and, as work progresses, simply remove the top layer of paper to give you a fresh, shard-free working surface.

Make sure there are no undue lumps and bumps as you prepare your working space, because glass lying unevenly places uncontrolled stress on the sheet. It is also handy to ensure you have enough room for all the tools you will need. They should be placed within easy reach, as you will need to get at them quickly.

ANGLE OF GLASS CUTTER NEEDED FOR VARIOUS THICKNESSES OF GLASS

thickness of glass degrees	angle
2–3 mm	120
2–6 mm	135
6–10 mm	145
6–15 mm	155
10–19 mm	157
19–25 mm	165

The glass cutter wheel has an angle to it where it comes into contact with the glass. This should vary depending on the thickness of the glass sheet. Diagram by Takako Tucker

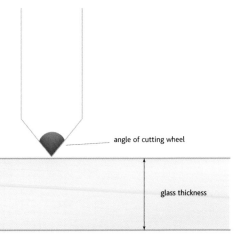

angle of cutting wheel

glass thickness

Making a straight cut

Hold the cutter along all three knuckles of the first finger. Secure with the thumb and second finger. This provides a very secure grip.

Hold the cutter upright on the glass. With an even pressure pull the cutter towards you.

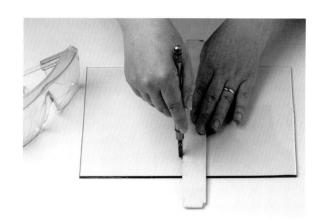

Position the cut spreaders on the score and apply pressure and the cut will open.

Photographs by Andrew Pritchard

Making a curved cut

The cutter is held in the same way as for a straight cut. Move the cutter towards you, following your design carefully.

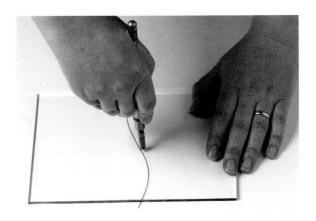

Using the ball end of a cutter, tap on the underside of the glass following the score.

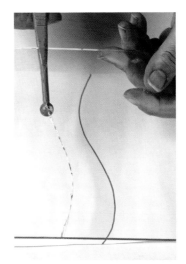

Continue tapping until the score line opens.

Photographs by Andrew Pritchard

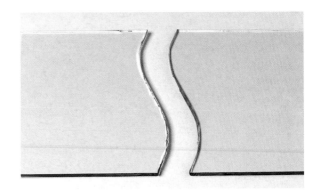

Cutting a circle out of a piece of glass

A

B

1. *Using a circle cutter score a circle to the required diameter (A). Using the ball end of a cutter, tap on the underside of the glass until you see the crack has moved round the entire circle. The glass disk will remain firmly in place at this stage, but it is important that the crack is complete.*

2. *Turn the glass over and make a series of scores (B) from just outside the circle to the edge of the glass sheet. Tap the glass from the underneath with the ball end of a cutter and watch carefully to run the scores into the circle score. If the scores (B) have been done at an acute enough angle to the circle (A) the tension in the glass automatically pulls the crack into the circle. This is why it is important to fully open the circle score.*

A

B

3. *As the pieces are tapped they will loosen and begin to fall away from the circle. Continue until all the pieces have been removed.*

Diagrams by Takako Tucker

Cutting a hole in a piece of glass

A

1. *Using a circle cutter score a circle to the required diameter (A). Using the ball end of a cutter, tap on the underside of the glass until you see the crack has moved round the entire circle.*

B

2. *Turn the glass over and make a series of scores (B) inside the circle, none of which should touch the circle. Tap on the underside of the glass using the ball end of a glass cutter to open up the scores. The trick is to get one piece out then the rest will follow quite easily.*

A

3. *Continue until all the pieces are removed.*

Diagrams by Takako Tucker

Cutting thin strips

It can sometimes be difficult to cut consistent thin strips from a piece of glass. If a series of strips are required, it is helpful to calculate the total width of all the strips and measure a piece of sheet which is either four or eight times that size. It should always be possible to cut the glass in half, so a piece of sheet six times the width of the strips required would not work. Once the glass is measured and cut to a width that is four times the finished size of each strip, score and cut the glass in half. Then take the two pieces, and score and cut them in half so that you have four pieces, all of the same size and length, cut to the required width. A glass score will always move towards the side where there is less glass, so keeping the sides to an equal size as you cut them will encourage the cut to run straight down the middle. Some very fine strips can be cut using this technique.

Cutting with a glasscutter is by far the quickest method, though some designs may require a little more shaping. A grinder is very useful for shaping sheet glass. It will refine an edge with a great deal of accuracy and is commonly used in the stained-glass industry. A grinder can be of

Kristal 2000 glass grinder.
Photograph provided by Creative Glass

great help for fitting pieces together. **However, you should always wear protective goggles while grinding and ensure the grinding head is lubricated with water to prevent glass dust escaping into the air.**

CUTTING USING SAWS

When a piece of glass is too thick or too textured to be cut by hand, or the design required is too intricate, a diamond saw is often a good option. Saws come in three main types: circular saw, band saw and ring saw.

Circular saws will only cut in a straight line, and are very useful for preparing sheet from fused blocks. Some circular saws need the glass to be rested on a sliding platform and fed in by hand. Others will have a facility to clamp the piece into position and for the glass to be fed in automatically. Both have their advantages, and it will depend on the work

Diamond circular saw.
Photograph provided by Creative Glass

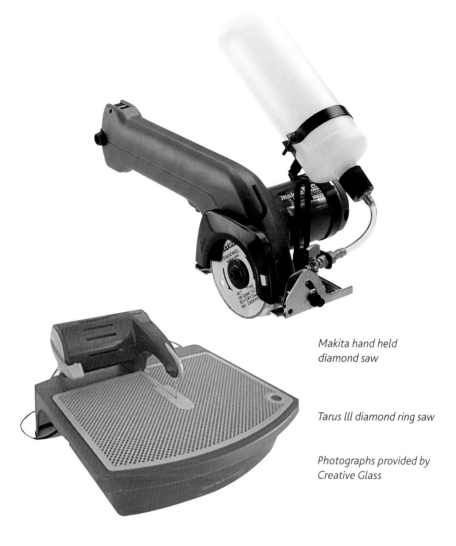

Makita hand held diamond saw

Tarus lll diamond ring saw

Photographs provided by Creative Glass

to be cut as to which is most appropriate. Band saws have a flat blade with diamond on one side. They allow for some manoeuvring, but are not as flexible as a ring saw. A ring saw has a blade that is non-directional, allowing it to turn through 360 degrees. This can help to develop intricate curves. It often has blades, which split and give the option of making inside cuts from a drilled hole with no trail cut (see Chapter 5: Slumping – Debbi Collins uses a ring saw to cut out her piece prior to slumping on p.48). All the saws will need lubrication. This would usually be water, but some circular saws use oil. Goggles should always be worn when cutting with a diamond saw or clamping glass into position.

Most of these saws are relatively expensive, but there is also a range of tile-cutting saws - which have diamond blades and water-cooling facilities - at reasonable prices in DIY stores. Always check with the manufacturer that their product is suitable to use with glass.

All these saws are great for processing larger pieces of glass prior to firing. When working on a smaller scale, most of the processes performed by the larger saws can be carried out very successfully with a flexi-drive, or hobby drill, with the addition of a few well-chosen diamond burrs.

The glass should always be worked with water to cool and lubricate it. Some makers prefer a drip system, which introduces a steady drip of water onto the glass at the point of cutting. The piece can also simply be held under water in a container. Don't let the drill head go in the water as it will shorten the life of the tool. When using any electrical equipment in this way ensure the manufacturers recommend its use with water in case of electric shock. Set up your work station well away from electric points so as to avoid splashes, and always wear goggles and protective clothing.

4. Fusing

What is fusing? Charles Bray describes the process in his *Dictionary of Glass* as 'the process of heating pieces of glass until they fuse together'. This quote sums up the technique perfectly. It is a very simple description for what can be a very simple, yet effective, technique. The process involves heating glass until it is soft and viscous enough to stick. It's a great technique through which to start learning about kiln-formed glass, as it's relatively easy to see the effects of the firing. This makes it possible to distinguish the various characteristics of the glass itself.

HEAT AND TIME

Both heat and time play an important role in the process of fusing glass. It's important to remember the basic properties of glass, as each different type reacts individually to heat in the way it softens, fuses and changes colour, and in the time it takes to do this.

Fusing can take place at a range of temperatures, and can result in anything from a tack fuse at lower temperatures, to a full fuse at the higher end of the heating scale. A tack fuse has occurred when the shape of the pieces of glass is retained but they have fused sufficiently to become a single solid piece; whereas in a full fuse the pieces of glass have fully melted together and all edges have completely rounded off.

The specific temperatures needed for a tack fuse, or for a full fuse, will depend on the glass being used and the kiln being fired. The information needed to determine which temperature should be used to fire the glass can be obtained from test strips. But it is not only the temperature that can affect the fuse. Time is also crucial. The amount of time for which a piece is held at a particular temperature has a major impact. If a tack fuse is required, it is often better to hold the kiln at the lower end of the fusing range, though for a longer period. This should maintain the crispness of the edges and yet make a strong join. The sharp edges of glass will begin to round off once the softening point has been reached.

Fused glass pendant by Kathryn Wightman

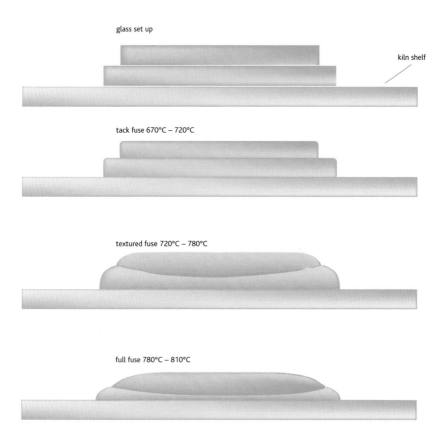

glass set up

kiln shelf

tack fuse 670°C – 720°C

textured fuse 720°C – 780°C

full fuse 780°C – 810°C

Fusing temperatures. Diagram by Takako Tucker

At the higher fusing range joints will merge more easily and layers of glass will become more fluid.

The peculiarities of each kiln will also play a part in the balance between heat and time. It's a good idea to carry out several tests first. When doing this, always keep consistent records to support your work.

LAYERING SHEET GLASS FOR FUSING

For the fusing process, glass can be stacked in a number of layers. The exact number of layers used will influence the result. Glass, if left to its own devices during a full fuse, will spread, or contract, to form a 6 mm (0.2 in.) thickness. This is related to its viscosity and surface tension. It is a very useful characteristic, which enables a certain degree of predictability when designing pieces. If, for example, you stack two 3 mm (0.1 in.) discs to make a 6 mm (0.2 in.) stack, the diameter of the piece stands a good chance of staying relatively the same after firing. If, however, the stack of glass were three 3 mm (0.1 in.) discs, making a stack of 9 mm (0.4 in.), the stack would probably spread. If the stack consists of only one disk of 3 mm (0.1 in.), it may pull up and, as a result, its diameter would decrease. This shrinkage means it is not possible to butt thin sheets together and still get strong joins. So for glass which is thin, it is necessary to have overlaps. That isn't to say that if the process is carefully controlled, it can't be used to great effect for design purposes. The key is testing and experience. Being aware of this tendency of the glass to revert to its 6 mm (0.2 in.) 'default setting' can make designing a piece easier.

Finally, the glass does not necessarily have to be stacked flat; it can be layered on its side for various effects.

USING COLOURED LAYERS

It is possible to achieve wonderful colour combinations by layering. The translucent quality of glass makes it a perfect vehicle. When layering, and fusing, the top layer of glass will sink into the lower level and will therefore thin it out.

The subsequent dilution in the intensity of that layer can lead to interesting effects. Moreover, as with painting, colours can also be combined in many ways. The way the pieces are stacked will influence the final result after firing.

Once panels are fused, they can be cut, ground and refired to explore a range of design possibilities.

aapt#

TRAPPING AIR IN LAYERS

It is possible to stack the layers of glass deliberately to encourage air
pockets. This can be achieved by criss-crossing strips of glass between
solid sheets, or by drilling and engraving into layers and trapping these
between sheets. But the firings have to be monitored more closely when
you are planning to create air pockets, as it is easy to overfire.

FUSING USING DRY PLASTER

There can be some benefit to fusing with plaster powder, as it helps to
overcome some of the problems caused by the work being flattened by
gravity. If the piece is well set up, dynamic three-dimensional forms can
be achieved.

Method and preparation

The plaster is very fine and will prevent fusing if it moves between two
pieces of glass. This makes it imperative to seal all joints thoroughly with
either tape or wax. It's worth noting that the tape will always leave a
mark of some description on the glass, whereas wax, if applied well, will
be unnoticeable after firing. The piece must be set up carefully in the
plaster to ensure that there are no air pockets that the glass can fall into.
This can best be achieved by loosening the powder normally used in the
ceramic 'box' or saggar. An unglazed plant pot makes a good saggar.
Alternatively, the plaster can be removed and then placed carefully, but
firmly, around the glass object as it is put back in. It is essential to make
sure this is always done under extraction, while wearing a mask and
protective clothing. The glass piece can be completely covered, or partly
exposed, but it is important to note that any glass not supported will sag,
though this of course can be used creatively.

Fused brooch by Yoko Kuramoto

Models are made using plasticine.

Build walls around the model. Yoko Kuramoto has used cardboard milk cartons, supported with kiln furniture. Mix and pour in refractory mould mix. See recipe 3, page 69

Glass is prepared using kugler colour roundels and silver leaf cut to shape. The silver leaf is held in place using a water-based glue.

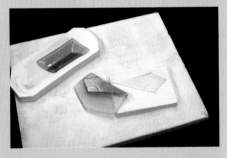

The layered glass is placed in the moulds and fired up to 760'c (1400'f) for the first firing. This firing fuses the glass and allows it to take up the form of the mould sealing the silver leaf in the glass. See firings, page 118

The shape of the glass is refined using a diamond saw.

The pieces are fired for a second time in the original moulds. This fire polishes and rounds off the edges.

The backs are ground lightly on a diamond flat bed and pins glued into place.

The finished pieces.

HEALTH AND SAFETY
- Always wear a mask when handling dry plaster.
- Use dry plaster under an extractor.
- Always wear an apron and remove it when leaving the studio.
- Never eat, or drink, while using plaster.

Removing the piece

When removing the piece, first spoon out the plaster. **Under extraction, wearing a mask and protective clothing**, place this onto newspaper. Remove all powder from the piece and wash it under water. Once the washing process has started, it is important to clean the piece thoroughly in order to remove any remaining plaster dust, as this could set hard in crevices and in any fine detail on the piece.

Plaster-fused ring by Yvonne Coffey

The glass is cut and ground to shape.

The piece is loaded into a terracotta flower pot with dry plaster (always wear a mask when working with plaster) and fired. The glass left exposed melts over the plaster. See firings, page 119

The front of the ring is ground and polished to create further contrasts.

Photographs by Andrew Pritchard

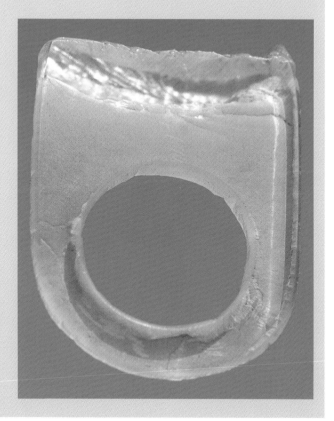

5. Slumping

Time and heat are elements that have an effect on making kiln-formed glass. However, when moving on to slumping, there is another variable to consider: that of gravity. This is because glass can also be shaped by being held in various ways: for instance, supported over a mould, or suspended, allowing its own weight to cause it to slump into a new form.

METHODS OF SLUMPING

- Into a mould
- Over a mould
- Through a mould
- Relief using ceramic-fibre paper
- By suspension.

The choice of method used in slumping will have implications for the qualities of the finished piece. Any of these methods can be used individually, or in combinations, to address particular design requirements.

INTO A MOULD

The mould will determine the final form of the glass, along with any textural qualities present. When slumping into a mould, the inside of the glass will be fire-polished, while the outside of the glass will take on the texture, and finish, of the mould with which it has been in contact.

A range of forms and moulds can be used to slump into. These can vary from found objects to tailor-made refractory moulds (See recipe number 1 p.62). Some can be used many times and are ideal for production work; but others are simply one-off creations for specific projects as in recipe number 1.

Slumping

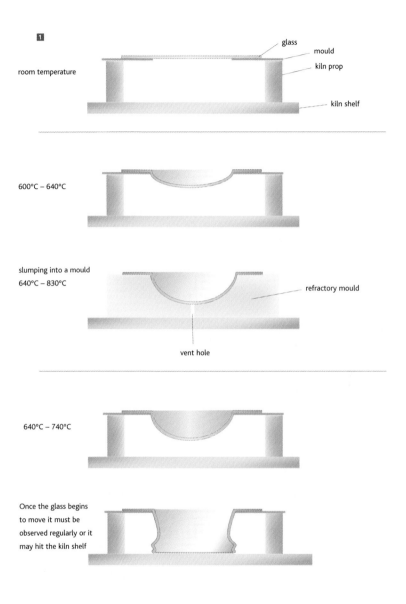

Slumping through and into a mould. Diagrams by Takako Tucker

43

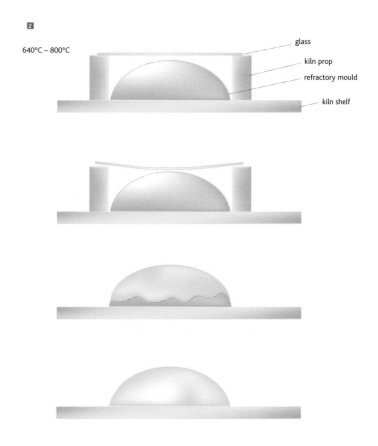

640°C – 800°C

glass

kiln prop

refractory mould

kiln shelf

Slumping over a mould. Diagrams by Takako Tucker

OVER A MOULD

As the glass is going over the mould, the inside surface of the piece will take up the texture of the mould and the outside will be fire-polished. For small pieces, it is best to place the glass directly onto the mould. With larger or longer pieces, the mould tends to create cold spots on the glass, and can result in cracking. To avoid this, support the glass just above the mould with kiln props, prepared with bat wash to prevent them sticking. The glass will begin to sag when it has reached its softening point, causing it to touch the mould and drop away naturally from the kiln props.

THROUGH A MOULD

The glass needs to be supported on the rim of the form through which it is going to be slumped. As the glass is heated, and softened, gravity will move it down through the hole. The length of time for which the glass is allowed to move will dictate the final curve of the piece. The glass will only be in contact with the mould on the upper rim, so both sides of the glass will be fire-polished.

METAL MOULDS

Not all metals will be suitable for use in the kiln at slumping temperatures of up to 840°C (1544°F). Both copper and aluminium will buckle and melt at these high temperatures. Stainless steel is a good choice, as it is able to withstand many firings, will not rust and is relatively light. Stainless steel can also be readily obtained on the high street in the form of domestic items. Note that metal will contract more than glass upon cooling, and is therefore likely to put pressure onto a fired glass piece if the sides are too steep. Only use a metal mould to slump into if the sides are relatively shallow.

Any metal mould will need a separator to prevent the glass adhering to it after firing. Ceramic-fibre paper is useful for simple forms, but bat wash is the most effective for more complex shapes, though it can be tricky to make it stick. Some makers will roughen the surface of the metal with a quick sandblast, or rub the surface with coarse sandpaper, before applying the wash. Applying the wash using heat is very effective in helping it to adhere. To achieve this, place your metal former in the kiln and raise the temperature to 230°C (444°F) over about 30 minutes. Then take out the mould and immediately brush the bat wash over the surface that is to receive the glass. If you want a smoother finish, the wash can be sprayed on, though you should **always do this in a spray cabinet using extraction and a respirator**. If you have not achieved a thick enough layer, the process can be repeated.

Slumped necklace by Amanda Simmons

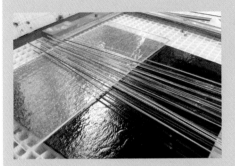

Using Bullseye fusing glass a sheet is fused with a black base layer, a clear top layer and stringers sandwiched between. The sheet is fired to a full fuse at 780°C (1436°F). See 'Firing', p.120.

Pieces are cut from the large fused sheet and set on moulds of fibre board rings. These are supported on kiln props. The fibre board is 10mm thick with holes of about 3cm diameter. The glass is fired to 720°C (1328°F) allowing the glass to slump through the hole in the mould.

The glass emerges with a range of characteristics.

The flanges need to be ground off to leave the slumped dome. This is achieved using a diamond grinding wheel.

The piece is worked with diamond pads, carborundum powder and finally it is polished. Holes are drilled into the piece with diamond burrs to accommodate the fixings.

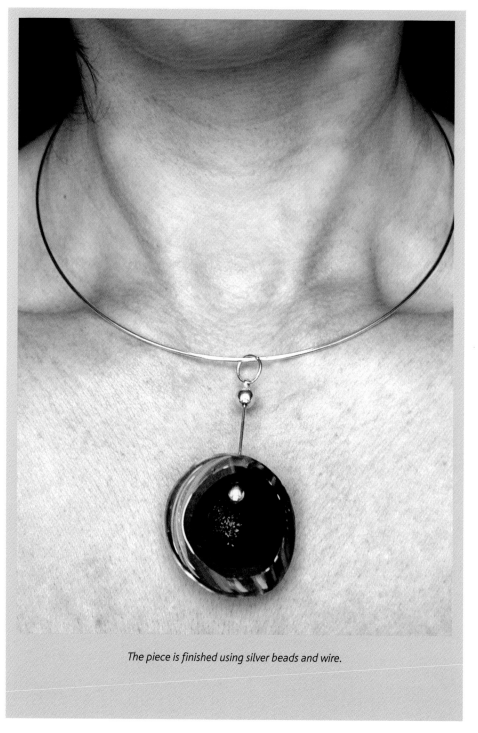

The piece is finished using silver beads and wire.

Slumping necklace using ceramic-fibre paper by Debbi Collins

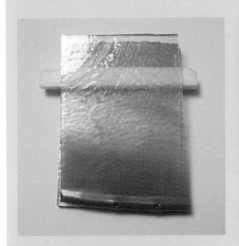

A strip of ceramic fibre paper is sandwiched between two layers of pink Bullseye fusing glass. The ceramic fibre paper is in position to form a hole for the chain of the necklace. The blank is fired up to 780°C for a full fuse. See 'Firing', p.121.

The fused blank is cut to shape on a non-directional diamond ring saw.

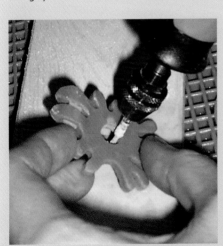

A hole is drilled and opened up with a flexi drive and a range of diamond burrs.

Ceramic fibre paper 3 mm thick is glued on to the underside of the armatures using PVA glue. Further ceramic fibre paper is put in the holes to keep them open during the second firing.

The prepared armature piece is placed on to a separately fired cabochon of clear dichroic glass with a cover of clear Bullseye for the centre detail. The whole piece is fired up to 750°C (1380°F).

The final piece has a high shine and rounded edges. The armatures are at varying heights because of the use of the ceramic fibre paper. The hole is threaded with a chain.

RELIEF USING CERAMIC-FIBRE PAPER

Ceramic-fibre paper and blanket are not only useful as separators. They are also ideal for use in relief work. Ceramic-fibre paper comes in a wide range of thicknesses and textures, and offers an exciting range of design possibilities. Forms can be cut out of the ceramic-fibre material using scissors, or a sharp craft knife. They can be built up directly on a kiln shelf. **Remember always to use gloves and to wear a mask and apron to protect against the fibres, as these can cause irritation.** When the design on the kiln shelf is complete, place the glass to be slumped on top of it. Next, fire to the temperature required. By balancing the heat and time, a range of effects can be realised. At the lower end of the temperature range, the glass will slump, but will not pick up all the

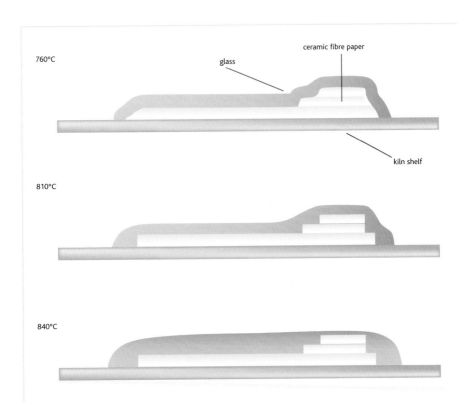

Slumping using ceramic fibre paper. Diagrams by Takako Tucker

angles and detail. As the temperature is increased, and the soak time is extended, the glass sheet will move more readily into the sharper angles of the ceramic fibre, but it will still retain the contour of the form. This in turn sustains the consistency of the colour. Once the temperature is increased even further, the glass becomes quite soft and surface tension causes the sheet to flatten out over the relief design. This will cause a disparity in the depth of colour.

SLUMPING BY SUSPENSION

Using this method, holes can be drilled into the glass. Then copper or refractory wire can be inserted and the whole piece suspended in the kiln. As the glass is fired and begins to bend, the wire will influence how the piece moves and curves. Some very subtle and interesting results can be achieved. Time and heat play a crucial role in this type of firing, and a close eye must be kept on the progress of the slumping in order to catch the piece at just the right moment.

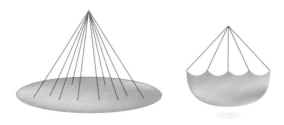

Slumping by suspension. Diagram by Takako Tucker

6. Gelflex

Gelflex is a rubber. It melts when heated and can be used for making the mould of a model with a range of undercuts. This avoids the need to make a complex multi-part mould. There are advantages and disadvantages to its use, though the pros far outweigh the cons:

Advantages
- It is reusable. The Gelflex can be remelted several times to make new moulds.
- Models with many undercuts can be removed from the Gelflex.
- Results contain a high reproduction of detail.
- It comes in two grades: hard and soft. These can be melted together to create the ideal rigidity for a particular project.
- It has a good shelf life.

Disadvantages
- It needs an accurate melting temperature.
- It must be poured hot. This means it is not suitable for all modelling materials.
- Good ventilation is required.

The two grades of Gelflex come in different colours, making them easy to tell apart. Also, both grades have slightly different melting points. As a rough guide, when selecting which grade to use, check whether the model has a lot of fine, delicate protruding elements. If this is the case, then the softer grade would be better, as it would make it easier to get these parts

Grade	Melting Point	Pouring Point
Hard: blue	160°C (320°F)	150–140°C (303°–284°F)
Soft: natural	150°C (303°F)	140–130°C (284°–266°F)

HEALTH AND SAFETY

• When handling Gelflex it is essential to wear gloves, goggles and aprons.

• It is best to establish a dedicated working area with good ventilation, extraction facilities and heat-proof surfaces. Ensure that all compound material is kept away from any food or any food-preparation areas.

• While melting, good ventilation and extraction is crucial to ensure fumes from the melting pot are not inhaled. If the Gelflex overheats, or burns, it will produce dense fumes. In this case, you should immediately turn off the melting pot, clear the area and allow the fumes to disperse completely, before cleaning the pot and disposing of the burnt compound.

• When Gelflex is in its molten state, it is much hotter than boiling water. This means that if it comes into contact with the skin it will stick, possibly causing serious burns. If this does happen then you should immediately hold the affected area under cold running water for at least two minutes then seek medical advice.

---

out of the final mould. If your model is thicker, and needs more support, then it would be better to use the harder grade. This is a rough guide, as not all models will fit neatly into these two categories. With experience, you'll find you are able to mix the two grades to suit whatever requirements are needed.

PREPARING THE MODEL

With the exception of wet clay, most materials require some preparation before being used with Gelflex.

Plaster, stone, cement
Water is an effective sealer for these materials. Soaking for 12 hours is usually sufficient. Make sure any surplus water is removed carefully before applying Gelflex.

Wood
There is no perfect sealant for wood, but as long as you take account of this in your planning, wood can still provide good results.

Metal

Aluminium does not require a release, but most other metals do. For fine finishes, 3-IN-ONE oil will provide the best results. For other finishes, varnish or shellac would work well.

Glass, china

It is not recommended that these materials are used if damaged, because of the heat required. They could pose a danger by either shattering or splintering into the Gelflex.

SETTING UP A ONE-PIECE MOULD

It is a relatively simple process to make a Gelflex mould of a shallow basic model. First, prepare the model appropriately depending on the material. Next, place the model on a board, build up the walls and seal with clay. Then heat and pour the Gelflex. Allow to cool, then remove it.

A model is made using clay to produce a Gelflex mould.

Clay walls are built around the clay model to hold the Gelflex.

1. Gelflex is cut into 1.5-cm cubes and placed in a heat proof glass measuring jug up to the half way line. Heat in two minute bursts following instructions.

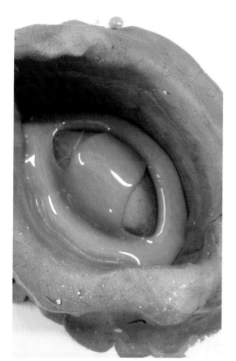

3. Remove the Gelflex from the model and clean thoroughly.

2. Pour the Gelflex over the clay model and allow to cool.

4. Melt the wax and pour it into the Gelflex mould.

HEATING GELFLEX

It is important to heat the Gelflex accurately, as overheating produces dense fumes, which pose a health-and-safety risk. Using a thermostatically controlled melting pot is one way to ensure a consistent melt. Always follow the health-and-safety guidelines and read the manufacturer's notes on how to use their products.

Easy steps for the perfect melt in a melting pot

- Cut the Gelflex into 1.5 cm (approx. 0.6 in.) cubes.
- Check the pot for old Gelflex and remove any residue to prevent burning.
- Set the appropriate melting point on the thermostat. See p.52 for temperatures.
- Place about a third of the cubed Gelflex in the pot if you are melting a full load, and replace the lid. Melting a little at a time allows for an even, steady heat. Stir regularly to distribute the heat.
- Check regularly once the melting process is almost complete. Then put in the next third and replace the lid. Repeat the process with the last third.
- Watch the melt closely to avoid any risk of overheating and burning, which could quickly result in the Gelflex being ruined and therefore becoming unusable.
- Even in a thermostatically controlled melting pot, it is still advisable to check the melting temperature regularly with a thermometer. This could also help avoid overheating.
- Once a full melt has been achieved, turn the thermostat to the pour temperature and allow the mixture to cool to that point.
- Under extraction, pour the Gelflex around the model. Take care not to incorporate air, or to pour it directly onto the model.
- Allow it to cool, then remove.

Melting using a microwave

First of all, never use the same tools or equipment you use to work with Gelflex with food. The microwave for Gelflex melting must be dedicated solely to that use and should be placed under an extractor to

remove the fumes of melting. As with the pot-melting method, heatproof gloves, goggles and apron are essential. If the Gelflex burns, follow the same procedure as for pot melting (see p. 53).

This is the method described to me by Angela Thwaites for her cast-ring project.

- Cut the Gelflex into 1.5 cm (approx. 0.6 in.) cubes and half-fill a glass Pyrex measuring jug.
- Set the temperature of the microwave on low, and microwave for two minutes.
- Inspect the Gelflex. No melting is expected at this stage. This is the initial heat stage. Close inspection must be maintained throughout the process to prevent burning.
- Place the jug of Gelflex back in the microwave on low power for a further two minutes.
- The Gelflex should be beginning to soften at this point. Each micro-wave differs, but by the time you have done a few melts the timing will become more straightforward. If the Gelflex has softened stir it gently and return it to the microwave. If it is still in cubes, microwave for another two minutes and stir once it has begun to soften.
- The heat can be increased to medium, but be cautious. Do not allow the Gelflex to change colour, as this is the first sign of burning.
- Keep heating and stirring the Gelflex in two-minute bursts until it is melted.
- Once the melt has been achieved, allow the Gelflex to stand in the jug for 30 seconds. This will allow any air bubbles to rise to the surface. Don't leave the jug of Gelflex to stand too long, as it is likely to cool down rapidly, making it difficult to pour.
- Under extraction, pour the Gelflex around the model. Take care not to incorporate air, or to pour it directly onto the model.
- Allow it to cool, then remove.

REUSING OLD MOULDS

The great advantage of Gelflex is that, as well as having an excellent shelf life, it can be remelted up to seven or eight times. But some attention must be paid to preparing the old moulds for optimum results. It is best to wash them using only mild, weak detergent. Dry the moulds thoroughly before reusing them. For the best results, cut the old Gelflex into small pieces, in the same way as you would for new compound, and melt as normal. As a rule, it is not advisable to mix old Gelflex with new. However, some manufacturers' guidelines state that it is acceptable to mix new compound with old Gelflex that has been melted just the once.

TIP

Gelflex, when melted, will cling to the inside of the pot and to any tools used for stirring. As a result, always put a little more mixture in the pot than required for the mould itself. It's not a problem to be a little generous, as the Gelflex can always be remelted if not required for this job.

---

7. *Small-scale Casting*

In this book, we have covered a number of ways of making glass jewellery. This chapter will focus on small-scale casting, which is one of the most flexible techniques for making three-dimensional forms. This is because it is possible to reproduce a number of different found objects, models, textures and colours with glass.

MAKING MODELS

Model materials

- Clay
- Wood
- Gelflex
- Wax
- Found
- Plaster

Clockwise from top left: plaster model, rubber mould, wax model, cast glass and finished piece by Antje Illner.

A range of materials can be used for the master: clay, wax, wood, Gelflex, plaster or found objects. The intricacy of the form you wish to cast will determine whether it is possible to make a refractory mould directly from it, or whether a Gelflex and wax should be made first. As the refractory mould is rigid, if an object has a lot of undercuts it will not be able to be removed from the cast mould. The only way to remove a model from the rigid refractory mould in this case is to melt it out, meaning that the model needs to be produced in wax. The ring project by Angela Thwaites (see pp.54 and 63) demonstrates the method for achieving this.

Clay is a versatile modelling material that can be used directly to make a refractory mould. The clay will allow for moderate undercuts, as it is pliable and can be dug out of the set mould, though this does mean that it can only be used once. If a series of the same form is needed, a Gelflex can be taken from the clay, and waxes taken from that for use with the refractory mould.

Once the model has been decided upon and made in the appropriate material, it is necessary at this early stage to consider how the glass will be cast into the refractory mould. The method for calculating the amount of glass required is covered later, but at this stage of mould-making decisions have to be reached as to how the glass is going to move into the mould. If the mould is very open, it is possible simply to set the model on a mound of clay before making the refractory mould.

This will become a fixed reservoir and will accommodate the glass to be cast in the kiln. If the model has one or more small entry holes for the

Cast and constructed ring by Emi Fujita

A range of reservoir setups

1. *Fixed reservoir*

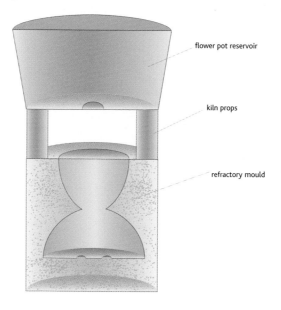

2. Flower pot reservoir positioned for dribble casting.

flower pot reservoir

kiln props

refractory mould

3. Reservoir with more than one hole to accommodate a more complex cast.

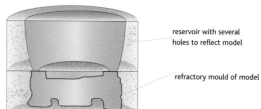

reservoir with several holes to reflect model

refractory mould of model

Diagrams by Takako Tucker

glass, a separate reservoir will be needed (see fig.3, p.61). This can be made by calculating where the holes need to be, modelling clay to reflect their locations, and casting a refractory mould. This will sit on top of the refractory mould for the model and can in some cases hold all the glass before firing. This separation of the glass can be useful if you are casting an intricate or fragile piece which would be damaged if the glass sat directly on it. Flowerpots make excellent reservoirs (see fig.2, p.61), the unglazed terracotta ones being ideal. Flowerpots come in a range of sizes with ready-made holes, and can be used several times if the same glass is being cast. However, they need to be rubbed down with wet-and-dry sandpaper to remove any rough flanges, which may inhibit the flow of the glass or may even shear off into the glass during firing.

MOULD MIXES

I have included a range of recipes to accommodate most needs, with reference to the most suitable applications and major properties. As you become more experienced, it will be possible to experiment with the information provided and to develop an individual approach.
When working with any dry powder, always work under extraction wearing a mask and an apron.

Recipe 1

Use for:
- Slumping into using sheet, strip, rod.
- Slumping over using sheet, strip, rod.
- Small shallow casts using float, beads, higher-firing glass.

Advantages	Disadvantages
• Ingredients readily available	• Not very strong
• Cheap	• Heavy
• No dry mixing	• Vermiculite can stick to glass
• Quick to make	when fired at higher
• Can be fired when wet	temperatures
	• The moisture in the mould will
	cause corrosion of the kiln

Cast ring by Angela Thwaites

Wax model carved with relief detail.

Wax model with reservoir and risers. Clay wall has been constructed ready for the refractory mould mix.

Ingredients for refractory mould mix before mixing.

Refractory mould mix poured over the wax model and allowed to set. When the mould has set thoroughly the mould is cleaned and the wax melted out.

Glass being measured using displacement of water. The glass is then loaded into the reservoir of the refractory mould for firing.

Refractory mould loaded with glass in the kiln ready for firing (see p.122).

The fired mould. The glass has flowed from the reservoir into the cavity left by the melted wax model.

The reservoir is cut off and the glass ground and polished. The refractory qualities of the polished bevelled glass highlight the details which were carved into the wax model.

| | | INGREDIENTS | | |
Water	Total weight of dry quartz ingredients	Plaster	Flint	Vermiculite
1 litre (2.1 pints)	1.5 kg (3 lb 5 oz)	750 g (1 lb 10 oz)	750 g (1 lb 10 oz)	($\frac{1}{3}$ by eye) of combined dry ingredients

Method

Measure out water into a clean bucket. Add flint by sprinkling it evenly over the water, then add the plaster, sprinkling it evenly as well. Allow the dry ingredients to moisten and sink into the water, then add the vermiculite. Using your hand, mix the ingredients beneath the surface of the water, to avoid any air getting into the mixture. The mix will start out the texture of single cream and should be ready to pour once it has reached the consistency of smooth runny custard. Being careful to mix at a consistent rate will enable you to sense when is the best time to pour.

Order of mix

You will notice that the ingredients are added in a certain order. Put in the flint first, then the plaster, followed by the vermiculite. There is good reasoning behind this order. Flint should be added first as it is inert in water. Plaster should be the second ingredient added as a reaction begins immediately the plaster hits the water, so you must act quickly. Vermiculite is the last to be added. It is very light and floats on water. If this were put in too soon it would create a barrier preventing the flint or plaster sinking into and reacting with the water. This would lead to a lumpy mix that would weaken the entire mould.

Understanding plaster

Plaster is quarried gypsum, which is ground and heated to remove the chemically trapped water. Because of this process, it is a material which is

Recipe 2

Use for:
- Slumping into using sheet, strip, rod
- Slumping over using sheet, strip, rod
- Detailed casts

Advantages
- Cheap
- Good for fine detail
- Strong
- Good release properties

Disadvantages
- Needs to be dry-mixed, requiring good extraction

		INGREDIENTS				
WATER	TOTAL WEIGHT OF DRY INGREDIENTS	QUARTZ	PLASTER	LUDO	CHINA CLAY	CHOPPED GLASS FIBRE STRANDS* LEVEL DESSERTSPOONS
0.5 litre	750 g	250 g	250 g	250 g	32.5 g	1
1 litre	1.5 kg	500 g	500 g	500 g	75 g	2
2 litres	3 kg	1 kg	1 kg	1 kg	150 g	4

Method

Measure out the water into a bucket. Weigh the ludo – ludo is old, fired refractory mould – and crush it into small bits. Crushed pieces should end up no bigger than 1cm (0.4 in.). Weigh all the other dry ingredients, then place the quartz, plaster, ludo and china clay in a strong sealable container that can be rolled. Roll the dry ingredients in the 'roller' until everything has combined. Sprinkle this dry mix over the water and allow it to settle. Let it stand to allow all the air bubbles to rise to the surface, and measure out the glass-fibre strands. Add these to the mix, and then, using your gloved hand, mix as you did recipe 1 (p.62) and pour in the same way. The procedure for cleaning is also the same for this recipe.

Recipe 3

Use for:
- Slumping into using sheet, strip, rod
- Slumping over using sheet, strip, rod
- Detailed casts

Advantages
- Does not need weighing
- Cheap
- Good for fine detail
- Strong
- Good release properties

Disadvantages
- Needs to be dry-mixed, requiring good extraction

Method

Under extraction, mix all the dry ingredients together thoroughly in a sealed container or roller. The china clay needs to be measured out conservatively, as too much can lead to an increased risk of devitrification. Measure out the water and sprinkle on the dry ingredients, allowing them to be thoroughly immersed in the water. Mix thoroughly as for recipe 1 and pour the mix round the model when it is ready. The removal and clean-up remain the same as in the two previous recipes.

Ingredients

The ingredients are mixed by volume and not by weight, so the size of the mould required will dictate the size of container used to measure out the ingredients.

Water	Plaster	Quartz	China clay
1 part	1 part	1 part	a pinch

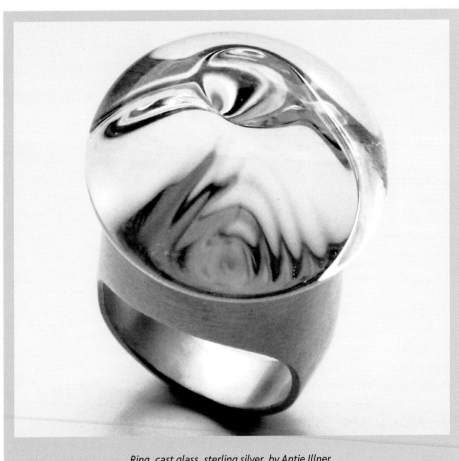

Ring, cast glass, sterling silver, by Antje Illner.

STACKING A MOULD FOR CASTING

Now you have your refractory mould and reservoir, you need to decide on the kind of glass you will use and how it should be loaded into the mould.

Firstly, you need to decide what form of glass to use. In addition to those factors already covered in Chapter 2, the form of glass will be largely determined by the end result you are aiming to achieve. This will become easier to determine and control as you gain more experience and build up good records of previous work. If you still are at the initial stages of discovery and feel this is a bit of a 'chicken and egg' situation, begin with small tests. Look at a range of work in the flesh, from which you will start to understand the making process of pieces you particularly like and the qualities you think would suit your work. Angela Thwaites has used a relatively large clear chunk of green Banas (see Suppliers' section) cullet for her ring, as she wanted a clear cast with good optical qualities.

You should certainly ask makers how they have produced pieces if you get the chance. Most makers are quite happy to share their methods. As you will see from the chapters we have covered so far, there are so many variables when working with glass. Each investigation into the making process is unique, and most makers are more than happy to let you in on a few trade secrets. The internet is very useful, with a lot of makers including details of techniques either on their websites or in information they provide to galleries.

CALCULATING THE QUANTITY OF GLASS FOR A CASTING

The type of glass chosen will determine the method you use to calculate the quantity required to fill the mould for casting. A simple method of calculating the quantity of glass required is to fill the mould cavity with water to the level you want the glass to achieve. Do this immediately after it has been made and cleaned. Half-fill a bucket (or measuring jug for smaller quantities) with water and mark the level. Pour the water from the mould into the marked container and mark the new higher level. Now pour the water out of the container back to the original lower level.

Fill the bucket with your selected glass until it again reaches the top mark. The glass that is in the water will be the same volume as the water originally in the mould. This method works well for larger frits, cullet slabs and ingots, but for powders and fine frits the disadvantages are obvious. For these forms of glass calculating by weight is more appropriate.

To calculate the weight of glass, fill a measuring jug to the top of the scale and note the amount of water, e.g. 1000 ml (34 US fl. oz). Pour the water into the mould cavity to the level you want the glass to reach. Note how much water is left in the jug, e.g. 350 ml (12 US fl. oz). Take this amount from the original 1000 ml (34 US fl. oz), and you are left with 650 ml (22 US fl. oz). This is the volume of water in the mould. At this point, you will need to know the specific gravity of the glass you are using. This is defined as the ratio of the density of a given substance relative to the density of the same volume of water, and is usually available from the supplier or manufacturer. Multiply the quantity of water (650 ml/ 22 US fl. oz in this example) by the specific gravity of the glass to be used, e.g. 2.5. Thus 650 X 2.5 = 1675 g (3 lb 11 oz) weight of glass.

The size of the glass pieces will influence the final transparency of the piece. The larger the piece of glass, the clearer the final cast. The finer the frit, the more opaque the result. Glass can be loaded in sheet, rod, stringer, bead and ingot form to mention but a few, or any combination of glass available. As long as the glass is compatible, it is suitable for loading into the mould. Some glass is better suited to certain fine and detailed casting. This tends to be the softer glasses and the ones which melt at a lower temperature. Experience will teach you which types and forms of glass best meet your individual needs.

CASTING WITH COLOUR

When you are using coloured glass, there are various ways a reservoir can be stacked. A certain amount of predictability can be obtained by observing the order in which the glass moves through the hole in the reservoir into the mould cavity. If you imagine the fall of sand in an egg timer, it is the top layer which gets pulled down rapidly through the hole. This is similar to the glass passing through the hole in the reservoir into the mould. The colour order in the reservoir will determine the final order of colours in the cast piece. Transparencies of glass can also be controlled in this way by positioning various frits, powders or ingots in certain places in the reservoir.

Cast glass from a flowerpot dribble cast. Glass powder was painted onto clear glass ingots. Layers can be seen where the clear glass and powder have interleaved in the dribble process.

1

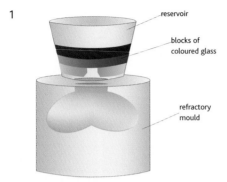

reservoir

blocks of
coloured glass

refractory
mould

2   Glass blocks painted with glass powder   glass ingots

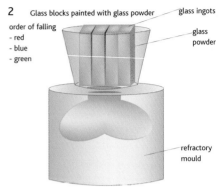

order of falling
– red
– blue
– green

glass
powder

refractory
mould

3   Combination clear cullet blocks
with coloured glass powder

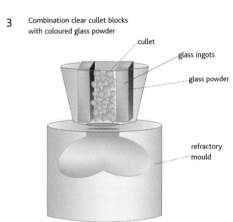

cullet

glass ingots

glass powder

refractory
mould

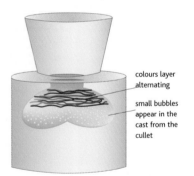

colours layer
alternating

small bubbles
appear in the
cast from the
cullet

1. *Colour flow from a reservoir into a mould. The glass will fall like sand in an hour glass from the centre to the outside.*

2. *Glass flow from a reservoir using glass blocks and powder. The glass will flow in an interleaving fashion forming waves of fine lines of colour in clear transparent glass.*

3. *A combination of cullet, powder and glass blocks. The cullet falls first, taking with it air forming small air bubbles. The glass blocks and powder follow and form a cap of interlaced colour floating in clear glass.*
Diagrams by Takako Tucker

As we saw in Chapter 2, glass can be purchased already coloured. There is more variety available now than ever before, but you are still restricted by what is on the market. Mixing your own colour could be just the solution for your piece.

Clear glass frit can be coloured by mixing it with coloured powder. This is done by percentage weight. If a 10% colour mix is needed then 9 g clear frit is mixed with 1g coloured powder. The intensity of the colour is determined by how much powdered colour is introduced along with the thickness of the final piece. A great pallet of colours can be achieved. Powders can be mixed before being added to the clear frit for added variations.

When the powder is added to the frit the tendency is for the smaller particles to move to the bottom, which will cause an uneven colour flow.

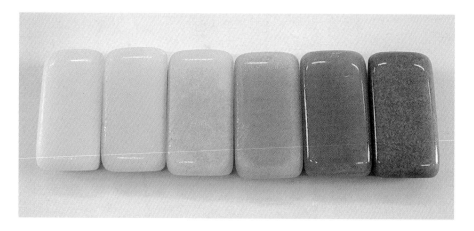

Coloured powder and frit percentage tests from left to right: 1%, 3%, 5%, 10%, 20%, and 50% coloured powder to clear frit.

HEALTH AND SAFETY
When using any glass powder always wear a mask and an apron, and observe good studio hygiene, clearing up any spills.

To overcome this, place the weighed clear frit in a small transparent polythene bag. With a water spray lightly cover the inside of the bag. Close the bag with a twist, trapping some air in it to create a bubble. Shake the bag to evenly coat the frit with the water. Open the bag again and put in the weighed coloured powder. Close the bag again as before, creating a bubble, and shake the contents to combine them. Use immediately to ensure the powder remains on the frit and an even colour is achieved. Only add water when combining powder with frit; if powder is being mixed with powder they will combine well when dry and adding water will only clog the mixture. Powder and fine frit can be applied to the surface of glass blocks before these are loaded into the reservoir. Tests are very useful in determining which colours and frits work best. If the percentages are weighed accurately, these can be scaled up properly for the larger pieces. Tests can also be carried out on various powder and frit sizes within a single firing.

Clear glass sheet with coloured glass powder

8. Cold-working

When it works, cold-working can completely transform a piece. Cold-working refers to processes such as grinding, cutting, engraving, shaping, sandblasting, polishing and cutting. All of this is done when the glass is cold.

Despite this, not all glass needs cold-working when it comes out of the kiln. Equally, you may find that the qualities you want for your piece can be achieved solely through cold-working, as with Rebecca Cheeseman's necklace (p.79). If this is the case, you may find that firing your work is unnecessary.

FLAT-BED GRINDING

When cold working, a flat-bed grinder is very useful for initially shaping a piece of glass. However, it will only grind flat or convex profiles, not concave ones. The aim is to shape the glass to the form you wish to fire or polish. To remove the glass as quickly as possible, you should use a coarse grit of 80 or 100 carborundum powder. As carborundum is 9 (out of 10) on the Mohs scale of mineral hardness, its hardness removes glass very effectively.

Flat beds consist of a flat horizontal disc of metal, which spins at a steady rate while being fed carborundum powder and water. The carborundum paste falls down a chute onto the revolving flat bed and is moved across the disc by centrifugal force.

Glastar B21 flat bed grinder.
Photograph provided by Creative Glass

> TIP If you are going straight to cold-working and have not fired the glass yourself, make sure it has been properly annealed.

The glass is then introduced onto the disc and is moved from the centre to the outside area, as it is ground and worked into its desired form.

WORKING AT THE FLAT BED

When working at the flat bed, it is best to stand comfortably with one foot in front of the other. When moving the piece on the flat bed, move from the hips and aim to maintain an even angle with your hands. To help maintain even grinding, turn the piece through 90 degrees after every two or three grinds to the centre. This helps maintain an even, flat surface. If you stretch too far with your arms, it is all too easy to start rocking the piece being worked and so distort its shape. Regular checking of the glass will let you know if you are on the right track and if any adjustments are needed.

It is also important to maintain the right proportion of carborundum and water. The water lubricates and cools, while the carborundum grinds. Too much water and the carborundum grit is thrown off the disc too quickly. With no grit, the glass can grip the disc, pulling it from your hands and throwing it off. This could cause injury as well as damage the piece. There should be a steady drip of both water and carborundum powder to create an even covering on the disc. In this regard it helps to dampen the powder before you place it on the chute. Obviously, the larger the piece being worked, the more water and powder will be required. Always wear goggles and a waterproof apron when working at a flat bed. Ensure all loose clothing and long hair is tied back when using machinery.

LINISHER

An alternative to using the flat bed, the linisher is a machine that can accommodate a range of vertical belts in various grades ranging from 80

Necklace by Rebecca Cheeseman. Sheet glass cut to shape, cold worked, drilled and mounted using rivets on a silver necklace. The rivets allow the pieces to move so the light throws the colours in different ways.

(very coarse) down to 600 (very fine), as well as a cork belt for finer finishing. This very much echoes the grits used in hand-lapping (see below) and for the flat-bed grinder. The linisher does the same job in that the aim is to refine the surface of the glass, initially by shaping the piece and then polishing it to the desired quality. It is of great use when working convex surfaces or edges. Because you are offering your piece to a vertical surface for working, you will find you can exercise much more control, as the area being worked is constantly visible. This is different from the flat bed, where all the grinding takes place underneath, out of sight.

The belts are tensioned on two drums. As with every machine, you should make sure you are familiar with how the linisher works; correct tensioning of the belts is important for safety as well as for successfully working the glass. The glass is water-cooled and, as with the flat-bed grinder, getting the correct flow of water is important. Different glass, and different sizes and shapes all have an impact on how the linisher needs to be set up, so seek advice from the experts. As with the flat bed, it is essential that you wear goggles and an apron.

Once you have established the form of your piece, the next stage is to hand-lap.

HAND-LAPPING

This technique also uses carborundum powder to gradually grind the glass through several grit sizes – 220, 320, 400, 600 – to prepare it for polishing.

Having finished on the flat bed, thoroughly wash the glass piece, your apron and your hands. Place the piece on a fresh sheet of newspaper or a paper towel.

I can't emphasise enough how important it is to be obsessively clean while polishing. To ensure a clean working situation consider the working environment. This should include level work benches that are easy to wipe clean. There should also be running water with a large sink, loads of clean newspaper, and good lighting using daylight bulbs.

PREPARING THE GLASS PIECE FOR HAND-LAPPING

Marking up your work with an indelible marker will help you see what has been ground and what needs further work. Wash and dry your piece, then use the marker to cross-hatch all the areas to be ground. This ensures that, when the piece is wet, it's easier to see if more work is needed.

BEVELLING EDGES

Glass does not like to be ground to 90 degrees. So it is always necessary to remove any sharp angle to prevent chipping. To do this, use a coarse diamond pad with water, moving it over the edges at an angle of 45 degrees.

THE HAND-LAPPING PROCESS

Hand-lapping grinds the glass finer and finer using successively finer carborundum grits ranging from 220 to 600, as follows:

1. Select a piece of float glass at least three times the size of the piece to be worked. The piece will be turned on the glass and therefore must not go over the edge.
2. Under good lighting, prepare an area of workbench with a wad of evenly spread newspaper, avoiding folds under the glass sheet.
3. Wash the glass sheet thoroughly. Do not wipe it dry, as this can introduce contamination. While washing, make the final rinse of the sheet glass under running water and move it from one side of the glass to the other. Hold it up briefly to drain and then place it straight onto the waiting newspaper.
4. Sprinkle 220 carborundum powder onto the middle of the glass.
5. Using a water spray, spray water onto the carborundum powder to create a paste.
6. Pick up the glass piece to be worked. Wash it under running water and bring it over to the float-glass sheet. Place it on the carborundum paste and start to make small circular movements, gradually moving in larger circles around the glass. Once the grit is more evenly distributed, you can pick up the speed a little. Check on the progress regularly, as the glass can be worn away quite quickly. (Continued on p.84.)

Cold-worked necklace by Yvonne Coffey

2. Photocopy the design and glue it onto the glass using solvent cement glue. This is used for bonding plastic plumbing pipes. The glue works well as it makes the paper temporarily waterproof enabling the design to be cut out on the ring saw. Cover the glass with a layer of glue, then apply the photocopied design and brush over another coat of glue. Allow to dry thoroughly before cutting.

1.Slice a lead crystal block on a circular diamond saw.

3. Cut out using a diamond ring saw. Drill a hole in the centre to access the middle.

4. Refine the shape using diamond wheels, burrs and flexi drive.

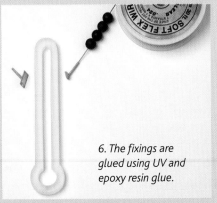

5. Grind and polish using carborundum powder (from 220-600). Make your own tools to fit the shape of the piece and use for the hand lapping process (see p.84).Finish by polishing with pumice and cerium (see p.85).

6. The fixings are glued using UV and epoxy resin glue.

Photographs by Andrew Pritchard

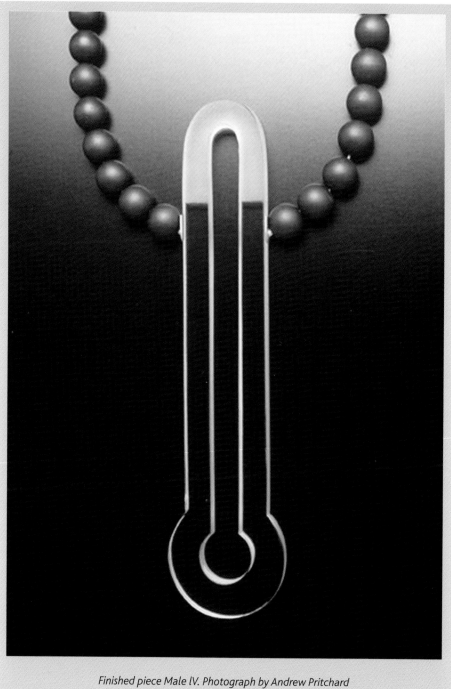

Finished piece Male IV. Photograph by Andrew Pritchard

7. Once you are satisfied that all areas have been ground satisfactorily, wash the piece thoroughly and place it on clean newspaper.

8. Repeat the process from step 3 onwards, using 320, then 400 and finally 600 grit. Don't forget to check the edge of the glass on a regular basis and cross-hatch each time. Also, remove a layer of newspaper to reveal a clean sheet for each new grit.

9. Once the piece has been ground to 600, it is ready for polishing.

MAKING YOUR OWN TOOLS

I have found that when making glass jewellery the right tool for the job is not always commercially available. This means that you may have to improvise and make your own. You'll find that when trying to refine small concave areas, often the best solution can be to make your own tool. If you can cut and grind a piece of float glass to fit accurately into a particular curve, you'll find that this is time well spent that will give you a consistent shape with which to form your piece of jewellery.

Steps to making your own tool for hand-lapping – grinding a torpedo-shaped slot

• Measure the size of the slot and select a piece of float glass that is slightly narrower. If you can't find anything that narrow, then go for the next size up and grind down evenly on the flat bed until it moves easily through the slot. The aim is to keep this tool as accurate as possible, so in this case you should take extra care to keep the two sides parallel, which will help you to make the finished pieces more consistent. If the tool doesn't accurately reflect the shape of your finished piece, you may find you are constantly checking the progress and adjusting your work, which takes time and could lead to unwanted inconsistencies in the finished piece.

• Once you have attained the correct thickness, focus on the curve of the torpedo. The aim is to make the curve echo the final shape of the piece you are grinding. This is a matter of judging by eye and checking regularly. A tool that is too pointy or too blunt will affect the final piece, making it a real struggle to achieve the shape you want for your work.

• The tool needs to be a good fit, but not too snug, as this will not allow for movement and could lead to the piece cracking or chipping. This tool should be used for the whole hand-lapping process from 80 grit down to 600.

• Once the tool has been formed, it is used with the grits which are applied to the tool in the form of a paste and used to grind the glass.

DIAMOND PADS

Diamond pads are used to remove areas of the glass and refine edges, and they can also be used for some of the stages in the polishing process. They range from very coarse grades for quick, effective removal of glass, to very fine powder grades intended for fine finishing and polishing. Pads come in a range of shapes and sizes, from thick, rigid blocks used to bevel edges, to thin, flexible sheets which can be cut to size. These allow access to small, awkward concave areas and can also be glued onto preformed wooden profiles to provide accuracy when working. This makes them particularly useful in the production of glass jewellery. The grade of diamond will usually be identifiable by its colour; although this grading varies from one manufacturer to the next, it is usually consistent within a given range and so will be helpful.

Always use the diamond pads wet. This provides lubrication and reduces dust. Glass dust is something to be avoided, so you should do whatever you can to limit your exposure to it. With this in mind, **always work wearing a waterproof apron that is easy to wipe down. Either work over a sink and regularly wash away slurry, or have a bowl of water on a pad of newspaper, change the newspaper regularly, and rinse your hands. Never let the slurry that accrues from the diamond pads dry out and begin to dissipate into the working environment.**

Polishing

After grinding the glass to 600 using carborundum powder and sheet glass, you can bring the glass back to a high polish through two further stages. The first is pumice on a cork wheel and the final stage is cerium on a felt wheel.

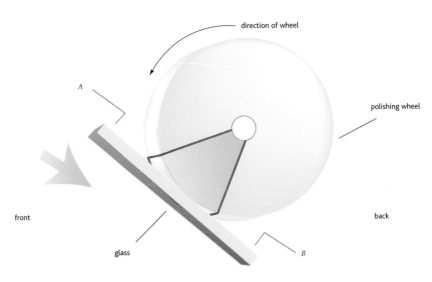

direction of wheel

A

polishing wheel

front

back

glass

B

The area which should be used for working the glass on a polishing wheel.
Edge (A) should not come into contact with the wheel as it can flip the piece away from the
wheel and can be dangerous. Diagram by Takako Tucker

PUMICE

The piece to be polished must be well washed and placed on a clean layer of newspaper. Position the cork wheel on the lathe. The pumice needs to be used wet and is best kept in a dedicated plastic container with a lid, along with a dedicated sponge for application. It is very important to keep your polishing materials uncontaminated so as to ensure a good-quality finish. If either pumice or cerium are contaminated then the whole batch will have to be disposed of, then the containers thoroughly cleaned and new sponges used.

Lathes vary in design and operation, so make sure you are familiar with the manufacturer's operating instructions. Always wear goggles and protective clothing, and tie back any long hair or loose clothing while using a polishing lathe.

> TIP Never allow the piece you are polishing to dry with the pumice slurry still on it. It makes the final cleaning much trickier, as slurry can set like concrete into small holes and crevices, and may refuse to budge even after lengthy soaking. A quick and effective method for cleaning out those small nooks and crannies is to use a plant water spray, as with the hand-lapping. It is best to have a spray dedicated solely for polishing.

Put the cork wheel onto the lathe. Before turning it, wet the wheel with the pumice slurry. Then put a layer of slurry onto the glass you intend to polish. Turn on the lathe and introduce the piece to the wheel. Work from the bottom of the piece to three quarters of the way up. **Avoid going too near the top, as if the wheel catches the top edge it will pull the glass from your grip and could cause you injury as well as damaging the piece.**

Only work on the section of wheel indicated (see p.86). This provides for optimum visibility and control. Once one end has been moved over the wheel three or four times, rotate the piece through 180 degrees. The same side is being introduced to the wheel, but now you are working the unpolished end. Now relaod the wheel with pumice slurry by soaking the sponge in the bowl, gathering up the wet pumice and holding it lightly to the rotation wheel until an even layer of moist pumice coats the surface. Further pumice slurry is introduced to the glass surface as before and the polishing is begun again.

Results should appear fairly quickly, which makes it an exciting stage in the cold-working process, as after much grinding you begin to see the internal movements and qualities of light being revealed. Checking regularly at this stage is important to ensure all areas are being evenly polished. Make sure that areas are not being overworked, creating grooves or heat. It is important to ensure that enough pumice and water are being applied, although bear in mind that the glass will always look more impressive when wet, so when checking the progress of the polish for quality and consistency, you should always dry the surface first.

When using pumice, there will always be a slight bloom with a faint bias to the shine. Only when you get to cerium can you expect a true crystal-clear shine. The aim of this initial pumice polish is to get a feel for the piece being worked and to take the frosted 600 finish down to the pumice stage. At the early stages of the pumice polish it is also to be expected that upon inspection some areas will still be a little frosted. It is worth marking these areas with an indelible marker, using dots or cross-hatching. Once the piece is wet, it can be quite difficult to identify the areas that need more work. Polish again, focusing a little more on the areas identified, and check as before when the piece is dry. If there are areas which need more work, go back to polishing until you are happy that a good, even finish has been achieved. All this will take practice.

Heat is always an issue when polishing. The pumice is using friction to remove a fine surface from the glass, and this inevitably creates heat. If the heat build-up is excessive, cracking may occur.

Avoiding heat build-up

- Keep polishing in short bursts with regular breaks.
- Use enough pumice slurry and water to assist cooling.
- Do not press the glass too hard against the wheel.
- Do not have the wheel on too fast a speed.
- If you do feel a build-up of heat, let the piece rest. Sit it on newspaper and leave it. Avoid plunging it into cold water, or throwing more pumice slurry onto it. This could cause thermal shock and create a crack.

Once you are happy with the quality of finish, thoroughly clean the piece and place it on a fresh piece of newspaper.

It is vital before you move onto the cerium stage that the glass is thoroughly clean with no pumice residue, otherwise streaks will appear on the final polished surface.

CERIUM

When moving from pumice to cerium, it is best to clear away all the pumice powder and wash all the surfaces and equipment before getting out the cerium. This will prevent contamination. Either invest in two waterproof aprons or thoroughly wash the one you have used for the pumice before you begin this next stage.

As with pumice, cerium is used wet. Again, it is best stored in its own dedicated plastic box with a lid and a separate sponge. Add water to the cerium powder until it has taken on the consistency of thin cream. Using the sponge, this should then be squeezed out onto a felt wheel. Before turning on the lathe, turn the wheel by hand, allowing the cerium and water to soak in.

The polishing process is the same as for pumice. Slurry is put on the surface of the glass and the piece is introduced to the felt wheel. Take care when using cerium, as it makes the glass very slippery. Once you are satisfied with the finish, clean the piece thoroughly, as the cerium clings and will find its way into all the crevices. If the cerium dries, just like the pumice, it will imbed itself and be very hard to fully remove.

COLD-WORKING AND POLISHING USING A FLEXI-DRIVE

A flexi-drive combined with a selection of burrs can do most of the finishing and cold-working jobs of the larger equipment (the lathe, linisher or flat-bed grinder). Felt, brush or impregnated rubber burrs can work very well for polishing glass jewellery. The burrs don't work so well for larger flat, even surfaces but are ideal for small intricate areas or concave surfaces.

The same basic principles of cleanliness, working environment and reducing cross-contamination apply when either polishing on a lathe or with a flexi-drive and burrs. The burrs are either felt, used in conjunction with pumice or cerium, or rubber impregnated with abrasive. Brush burrs can be used with pumice to create a subtle, diffused finish that can be particularly effective on textured glass.

A range of diamond burrs used by Emi Fujita

Use the flexi-drive on a slow speed and apply pumice slurry to both the wheel and the piece of glass. Move the wheel over the surface and regularly check progress. Keeping the wheel moving helps to prevent grooves forming. This is more of a danger here than with the larger wheel. If you need to polish a concave area, select a burr that suits the profile and do as above.

As with the larger wheels, to prevent contamination you should always have a dedicated set of butts for both pumice and cerium, along with lidded boxes for the slurry.

SANDBLASTING

Sandblasting is used to remove the outer layers of the glass. This is done by propelling abrasive powder under pressure from compressed air onto the work. The glass has a frosted appearance and, depending on how aggressively it is sandblasted, it is possible to create relief designs of various depths, or even go right through the glass.

If a particular design is required, masking off is necessary (see the section on masking agents, below). Once masked off, the piece is sandblasted. The finish after sandblasting is very susceptible to dirt and fingerprints, and will usually require further finishing. This can be done with acid-etching through dipping, acid paste, fire-polishing or brush-polishing.

MASKING AGENTS – WHAT CAN BE USED AND HOW TO APPLY THEM

Sticky-back plastic This can be purchased from hobby and craft shops and will do a very good job of masking off, even though it is of average quality. Alternatively, a much higher grade of sticky plastic sheet can be obtained from speciality glass suppliers. This is much heavier duty and is designed specifically to withstand prolonged exposure to sandblasting. It will give a much crisper line to your design. Either cut a shape out of the sheet, peel off the backing, and apply to the glass; or cover the entire glass piece in the plastic sheeting and, using a craft knife, cut out the design and remove the section to be sandblasted.

Masking tape A much thinner material, readily available, and easily applied. Although it will not withstand prolonged sandblasting, it can allow for a softer finish. Ensure the tape is well stuck down, as any bubbles at the edges quickly lift, which will cause the design to be compromised.

Electrical tape Very rubbery and flexible to apply, so ideal for complex three-dimensional forms. Withstands sandblasting and wet working well, and cuts smoothly. As with masking tape, ensure all the edges are firmly in contact with the glass, or the sandblasting will creep underneath.

PVA glue The glue is applied as a liquid and therefore offers a range of qualities not possible with sheet or tape. The glue can be applied directly from the container if this has a pointer nozzle, and can be used quite freely as if you were drawing with it. Otherwise, apply the glue with a paintbrush. Either neat or watered down, the range of qualities is extensive. The glue can also be applied with sponges, tools or even fingers. All these techniques can be experimented with until you develop a range of qualities which fit your requirements. Once applied, allow to dry thoroughly and it is ready to use. To remove, either peel it off or, if that is proving awkward, soak it in water for a few minutes, and the glue should begin to release.

All of these masking materials can be used separately, or in combination, and only by practice and experience will you become familiar with the endless creative possibilities. All these techniques can be applied before firing to achieve a wide range of outcomes.

DRILLING HOLES

You must ensure that you always lubricate glass when you are drilling. Use plenty of water, and make sure that the drill you are using is the right one for the job. To drill the hole, select a diamond burr which is spherical and the right size to make the hole you want. Using a low drill speed place the burr at the centre point of the hole to be drilled. Apply constant pressure so that the diamond can grind through the glass, being careful to pull back regularly to clear the hole of debris, then carry on. To avoid chipping, just as the burr breaks the underside of the glass remove the burr and turn the glass over. The small hole on the reverse can now be used as a guide to complete the hole. It is never advisable to drill tempered or safety glass, and you should never drill any glass too near its edges.

9. Fixings

It is important when you are still designing your glass piece to consider how it is going to be attached to the body, as this will affect the overall visual impact of the jewellery.

There are various ways of fixing jewellery, and a wide variety of materials work well with glass. There are some very good products on the market ready to buy and attach to your glass piece along with chains and brooch backs (see Suppliers p.126). However, it can be satisfying and sometimes aesthetically more appropriate to design and make your own fittings.

I have outlined below various solutions developed by individual makers for fixing their own jewellery.

Jed Green brooch BR10 The glass has been cold-worked from sheet and set using traditional silversmithing methods onto a fabricated silver brooch. The pin runs down the back of the main stem of the brooch.

*Jed Green
Brooch: BR10*

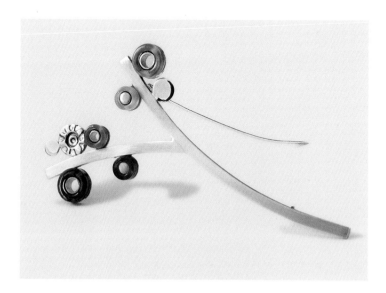

Fixings

Jed Green Necklace: N55.

Debbi Collins Necklace. Ceramic fibre paper is laid between the layers of glass before firing. This keeps the glass open at this point and creates a hole for the chain to be threaded through.

Antje Illner Necklace: Violet. The cast glass has a groove specifically incorporated into the edge to accommodate the linen thread.

Jed Green Necklace: N55 The glass has been cold-worked from sheet and rod. The ring has been set in silver and the rod has been glued to secure it in the silver collet, which allows it to be attached to the chain.

Debbi Collins Necklaces: For the necklace, two pieces of glass have been cut to shape. Towards the top, small pieces of ceramic-fibre paper have been sandwiched between the two sheets. This is to keep a hole open when the piece is fused. A smooth chain, or wire, is then simply slipped through for the necklace.

Antje Illner Necklace: Violet Cut and sandblasted lead crystal has been bound by crocheted linen thread.

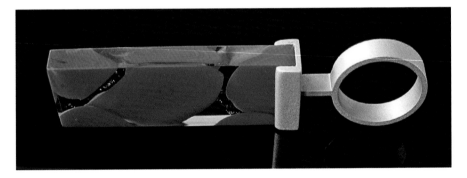

Zuzana Kynclova Ring 1. The glass is fused together, cut into slices and polished after cold working. Silver is cast into simple rings, shafts and slots. These are soulderd together and the glass is glued into position.

Zuzana Kynclova Ring 11. The glass is fused together, cut into slices and polished after cold working.

Zuzana Kynclova Ring 1 Static cast glass has been polished and glued into place. The silver has been cast and fabricated to form the ring.

Zuzana Kynclova Ring 11 Static cast glass has been drilled and cold-worked to form the ring.

Purple Jewellery by Storm Crystal forms are glued in place into prefabricated silver metalwork.

Purple Jewellery by Storm. Precision crystal glass is glued into intricate silver frames using UV glue. Photograph provided by Storm.

Yvonne Coffey group of necklaces Cold-worked lead crystal and small silver plates with tubes running up the bead have been glued together using Bohle UV glue type B 690-0. The silver tube running up through the beads is 2 cm (0.8 in.) long and has steel threading wire glued into it using an epoxy resin. The addition of heat increases the strength of the bond. The beads themselves had to be drilled to enable them to thread over the silver tube.

Yvonne Coffey group of necklaces. Hematite beads have been sand blasted and waxed. Silver tubes with plates soldered on are glued onto the glass piece using Bohle UV glue. Advice was sought from Bohle as the project required a high strength bond on a very small surface. The bond also has to withstand vibration and movement. The beads are threaded on to plastic coated steel wire. The ends of the wire are then glued into the silver tubes and allowed to set. Photograph by Joël Degen.

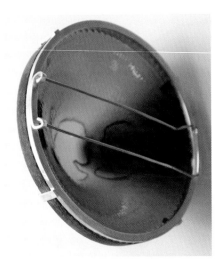

Tarja Lahtinen: Cameo Brooch
The brooch has had a setting made to fit the glass which has then been mounted. The double pin provides stability for the large disc.

Tarja Lahtinen: Cameo Brooch, back. The silver has been constructed and soldered to fit the recycled sandblasted glass. The glass is then set in the silver back using the traditional claw method where the silver spikes are pushed over the glass to secure it. The brooch is designed with a double pin for stability.

MAKING HOLES IN GLASS

There are several ways of making a hole in glass, which can then be used for inserting a range of threads, metals or pins to attach the glass to the wearer. Holes can be drilled, using a piller drill especially adapted for glass use. This works well for larger holes, and for rings or brooches, but when a finer hole is required, a diamond burr used in a flexi-drive is ideal. (See Chapter 8, Cold-working, p. 77)

Diamond burrs and drill used by Emi Fujita for constructed ring pieces.

If the glass is to be fired after drilling, the holes will need to be kept open. If the hole is the right size, this is usually done with soft pencil leads or graphite. These can be easily pulled out, or drilled, after firing. If the hole is larger, then ceramic-fibre paper can be used to fill it. Ceramic-fibre paper can also be used sandwiched between two pieces of glass, before the pieces fuse when fired to create a hole, as in Debbi Collins's piece on p.48. Alternatively, the glass can be built in three layers. A small section of the ceramic-fibre paper is laid onto a full bottom layer of glass, covering more than the full width of the glass so that it can be removed later. Then two further smaller pieces of glass are placed at either end of the ceramic-fibre paper on the bottom layer of glass. These pieces in turn support a final full sheet of glass on top. A hole will be created when the ceramic-fibre paper is removed after firing. Both pencil leads and ceramic-fibre paper can be used in casting as well to produce holes.

If the glass is being fused, and there is scope in the design, the glass can be laid on the kiln shelf in such a way that holes are created. Overlapped strips or frits can be stacked in this way.

BONDING OF GLASS JEWELLERY USING GLUE

Given the wide range of possible materials that can be used with glass, gluing can sometimes offer a very good way of solving fixing problems. Each project varies, so it is important to understand what glues have to offer when it comes to making technical decisions. Most glue manufacturers have very good technical support departments that are usually happy to give advice or to consult on specific projects. There are often optimum-fixing procedures, involving cleaning, heat application and curing conditions. These things can really improve strength and performance over time. Think carefully about the materials you are gluing and what you expect them to do. This will help you choose the right glue. You need to consider, among other things, whether the bond needs to be weight-bearing, transparent, flexible or moisture-resistant. Moreover, considering the way the glue needs to cure and what its properties are will help to match the requirements of your piece with the performance of a particular glue.

Curing mechanisms of some glues

Most glues are reactive polymers that change from liquids to solids through a range of chemical reactions. It is possible to define adhesives by their curing properties. This is also useful when deciding which glue is best suited to a particular task, as the conditions of curing will dictate the final strength of the joint.

The following are the main curing groups:
- Curing by anaerobic reaction (engineering adhesives)
- Curing by exposure to ultraviolet light
- Curing by anionic reaction (super glues)
- Curing using an activator system
- Moisture curing
- Heat curing.

Curing by anaerobic reaction
These adhesives cure at room temperature when deprived of oxygen. This can occur when two components are introduced to each other at the joint to be fixed. The curing component in the liquid remains inactive as long as it has contact with oxygen. The glue is quite runny, and this allows it to get into every crevice.

The curing process is speeded up by contact with metal, but with some materials an activator is required. In this case the activator is applied to either one or two sides before the glue is used. This acts as a catalyst and speeds up the curing time. There is no problem with pot life with this type of adhesive.
Materials which speed the cure: Brass, bronze, copper, iron, steel.
Materials which slow the cure and may need an activator: Aluminium, ceramics, glass, plastics, silver, stainless steel, tin, zinc.
Properties: resistance to vibration.

Curing by exposure to ultraviolet light
The wavelength and strength of the ultraviolet light will affect the quality of the cure. Ultraviolet light will vary in wavelength depending on the source. The UV curing process has two main areas to consider:

> **WARNING** The shorter UVC rays can be very dangerous, even causing blindness, so you should always use a special lamp designed for the purpose, including a safety lock.

Depth curing This is activated in the wavelength band from 315 to 400 nm, or UVA-light.

Surface curing: This is activated in the wavelength band below 280 nm, or UVC-light. If this wavelength is not used, the surface may remain tacky because of the reaction of the adhesive with atmospheric oxygen, which, as with anaerobic reaction, inhibits the curing process.

Properties: high strength, very short curing times, good environmental resistance.

Curing by anionic reaction

Anionic-reaction glues, commonly known as superglues, cure in contact with slightly alkaline surfaces. The humidity in the air and on the joint surface is usually enough for the adhesive to cure in seconds. They will also bond skin to skin in seconds, so great care should be taken when using them and you should wear gloves and protect your clothing. The moisture on the surface of the joint neutralises the stabiliser in the adhesive. So the curing takes place from surface to surface. It therefore follows that to achieve the fastest cure the smallest gap possible is desirable.

Properties: rapid curing, very high sheer and tensile strength, capable of bonding most materials.

Curing using an activator system

Activator systems cure at room temperature when used with an activator. The adhesive and the activator are applied separately to the surfaces. The curing starts when the two parts are joined.

Properties: very high sheer and tensile strength, good impact resistance, capable of bonding most materials, good at filling gaps.

Moisture curing

The main material used in this type of curing is silicon rubber. When moisture comes into contact with the silicon, it begins the curing process. Therefore, the curing takes place from the outside in and is limited to 10–15 mm (0.4–0.6 in.) depth. No special conditions are required; normal humidity is usually sufficient.

Properties: good heat and cold resistance, flexible and tough, good at filling gaps, excellent at sealing.

Heat curing

The temperature for curing will depend on the glue being used, for which the manufacturer's guidelines should be followed. The curing time is related to the temperature. Normally, the higher the curing temperature, the shorter the curing time. Some adhesives use heat curing as an additional cure mechanism.

Properties: medium to high strength, good at filling gaps, good environmental durability.

BONDING WITH UV CURING GLUE

UV curing glues are particularly useful for glass. There is a wide range on the market, but for the sake of clarity I am going to look more closely at just one range. Bohle have a wide variety of products, as do other glue manufacturers. There are four products I will look at in more detail, which can offer good solutions to most UV gluing problems. Bottles are supplied in sizes ranging from 1000 g (2.2 lb) down to 20 g (less than 1 oz). The availability of the smaller bottles is a great advantage to the glass jeweller. The glue has a limited shelf life and an old glue will not give the strongest bond.

With the different viscosities, final consistencies and suitability for different materials of these products, it is obvious that in order to make the right choice of glue, you have to consider the final requirements of the piece as well as the materials to be glued.

It is important to prepare the surfaces to be bonded. The curing mechanism of the UV glue is also anaerobic, meaning without oxygen, as with engineering glues. This dictates that the gap should be as small as possible so as to exclude air. Surfaces must be totally clean – free of

UV CURING ADHESIVES FROM BOHLE

Adhesive code	B-665-0	B-682-0	B-690-0	B-678-0
Final consistency	brittle	very hard	elastic	elastic
Bonding gap	0.1–0.2mm	0.1–0.5mm	0.1–0.5mm	0.1–0.5mm
Viscosity	low	medium	medium	medium
Suitable materials	glass to:	glass to:	glass to:	glass to:
	• glass	• metal	• glass	• laminated glass
	• wood	• wood	• wood	• wood
	• stone	• stone	• stone	• stone
	• some thermo-plastics	• some thermo-plastics	• some thermo-plastics	• metal
				• some thermo-plastics

grease, dust and moisture. Cosmetic glass cleaners are generally not appropriate to use as they leave a residue that will shine the glass and can interfere with the curing process. Bohle supply a cleaner specially designed for this task, which works well for their glues, making the glass literally squeaky clean. When using it, apply the cleaner in moderation to a lint-free cloth, which will not shed pile when cleaning. The less cleaner you use, the less there is to remove from the glass.

Be aware that moisture will inhibit curing. In this regard, applying heat will disperse any invisible condensation build-up on the surface. You can either use a paint stripper in a short sharp burst across small pieces of glass, or you can invest in the hot-air gun that Bohle produce, again expressly for this purpose. A hairdryer is not powerful enough to drive away the moisture. To avoid cracking, various shapes and sizes of glass will require slightly different approaches to heating. If the piece has not bonded within five minutes, the heating should be repeated. Apply the glue and expose it to the UV source. It is recommended that protective goggles including a UV filter are worn to protect the eyes.

Constructed cast-glass ring using glue by Emi Fujita

Right: The construction of a cast ring by Emi Fujita.
After pieces have been cast they are ground and refined using wet and dry paper and carborundum powder.

Far right: Once the pieces are fitting accurately, they are positioned and holes drilled using diamond burrs.

Right: The heads of small screws are cut off to make stabilising pins.

Far right: The pins are inserted into the holes along with an epoxy resin glue.

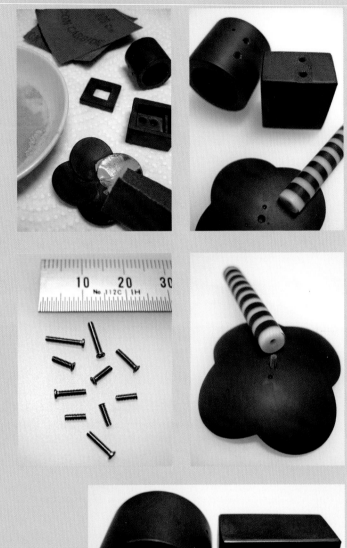

Pieces are slotted together carefully.

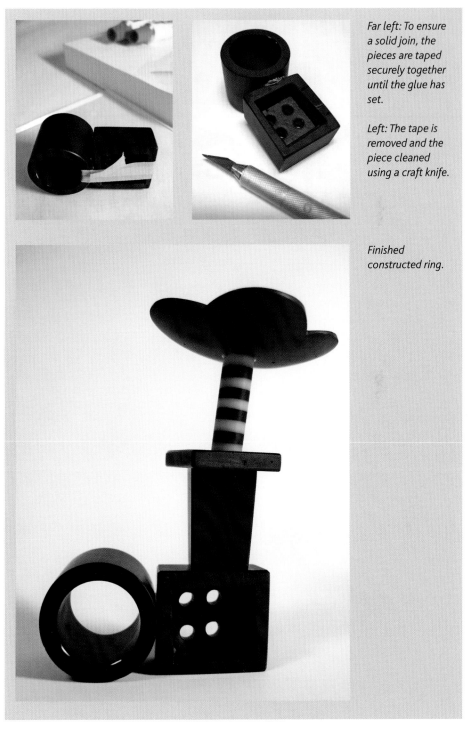

Far left: To ensure a solid join, the pieces are taped securely together until the glue has set.

Left: The tape is removed and the piece cleaned using a craft knife.

Finished constructed ring.

Curing is done in two stages. The first exposure is about 10 seconds and provides about 70% of the final strength. When the glue is in this state, any excess can be easily removed with the Bohle cleaner using fine wire wool and scalpel. The final cure is then achieved by further exposure to the UV light for between one and five minutes.

If the glass differs from straightforward float glass, with well-engineered surfaces that need to be bonded, the gluing process may vary. As a result, test-bonding is always recommended. Textured glass will be harder to glue as it tends to have gaps that allow oxygen in, which inhibits curing. Certain colours of glass will prevent UV rays penetrating through to the glue. Green glass, in particular, can be tricky.

As with glass, metals need to be cleaned thoroughly. Plating can be a problem – for example, silver plating, which has the potential to shear off before the bond itself gives.

10. Firings, Kilns and Annealing

FIRING CURVES AND SCHEDULES

The aim of a firing is to heat the glass to the necessary temperature to melt and alter the glass in the appropriate way for the piece. Control needs to be applied to the heating and cooling phases to avoid cracking, or stress, in the glass.

This is achieved by writing a firing schedule, which takes into account the peculiarities of the kiln, the shape of the piece and the characteristics of the glass being fired. Aspects such as size, shape, and type of firing (e.g. fusing, slumping or casting) need to be considered.

At the end of this chapter, I have outlined the firing cycles for all the projects featured in this book. I hope this information will allow for the structured development of your own personal approach. You'll find that hands-on experience will hone your practice and enable you to become familiar with your own kiln and its firing foibles.

STEPS OF A FIRING CYCLE

The firing schedule can be split into eight sections. Each has a specific role to play in the firing. Being aware of the various properties of these stages can help identify the cause of a problem if it occurs.

The eight stages are: initial heat, soak, rapid heat, soak at top temperature, crash-cool, anneal-soak, anneal-cool to strain point, and finally cool to room temperature.

Outlining the role of the eight phases of firing

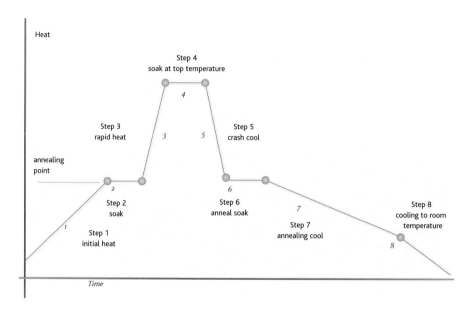

The eight phases of the firing curve. Diagram by Takako Tucker

Step 1:

The first stage is called 'initial heat'. The bung of the kiln should be out, to allow moisture and impurities to escape. This initial heat usually takes the glass up to the annealing point. This stage has to be followed with caution, so the glass does not crack. Consider the shape and size of the glass. Also, consider the shape and size of the kiln in relation to the glass. If you are fusing flat, long pieces and your kiln has side elements, go slowly. This is because the ends of the strips will heat rapidly and may shear off. If the same long pieces are in a kiln with elements only in the top, then a more rapid heat will be possible as the whole strip will heat evenly.

If you're casting glass using a large ingot then a slower initial heat is advisable, as again the glass may crack. This is because it won't be able to conduct the heat into the centre very successfully, as glass is a poor conductor of heat. It will also struggle to reach top temperature and thus to melt well. It needs time to fully heat through at this earlier stage. If the same casting is being filled with smaller cullet, a faster initial heat will be fine, as all the individual pieces of cullet can be treated as separate and should heat well.

Step 2: This is called 'soak', and is an optional part of the process that you should include when firing larger moulds or thicker glass. It allows everything to reach the same temperature before going into the rapid-heat phase. The soak is normally done at the annealing point of the glass by holding the kiln at the annealing point for a certain length of time. The length of time will vary depending on the project you are making.

Step 3. This is known as 'rapid heat'. If you are confident that all the moisture and impurities have burnt off, put the bung back into the kiln to contain the heat. The aim is to put as much heat as possible into the kiln to get to the top temperature as quickly as possible. The advantage of this speed is twofold. Firstly, the less time the glass spends above the annealing point, the less susceptible it is to devitrification. Secondly, glass cannot be cracked, and is not susceptible to thermal shock, above its annealing point. It is therefore an advantage to move as quickly as possible through the rapid-heat phase in order to save time and energy.

Step 4: This is called 'soak at top temperature'. Again, to retain heat, keep the bung in. Top temperature is the temperature at which the fusing, slumping or casting will take place. The heat will usually need time to do its job, which is allowed for in any soak time. Often the same effect can be achieved using a higher temperature and less time, or a lower temperature and a longer time. It can be interesting to experiment along these lines.

It is usual to visually inspect the glass at top temperature to check if it has achieved the desired result. Always wear safety clothing and thick heat-resistant kiln gloves, as well as protective goggles. If the glass has not melted to quite the required stage there is a choice. You can either extend the time you hold the glass at the top temperature or you can raise the top temperature by between 5° and 10°C (41° and 50°F). There is no single correct method – it depends on the kiln, the glass and the required result. In this regard, it is important to keep accurate notes as you are fine-tuning the firing in this way.

Step 5: This is known as the 'crash-cool'. Take the bung out to allow heat to escape. The reason for crash-cooling is to set the glass as you want it. This is achieved by opening the kiln and the vents, and allowing the heat to escape. It should be done in short bursts, with a close eye kept on the temperature readout, and the kiln should never drop below 80°C (176°F) above the annealing point.

For example, if the annealing point is 520°C (968°F), then the temperature should never drop below 600°C (1112°F). If the temperature plummets, and slips below the all-important annealing point, then the glass may become stressed and crack. The thermocouples, which relay the kiln temperature to the readout, are often at the back of the kiln (or at the bottom of a top-loading kiln). This means the temperature they read is higher than at the front (or top) of the kiln, where there is likely to be glass. This could lead to cracking if the temperature readout is followed too closely. So it is best to allow a margin of 80°C (176°F) to cover any discrepancies. Once the necessary temperature has been achieved, close the door and continue the firing.

The crash-cool has the benefit not only of fixing the glass, but of moving it more quickly through the potential devitrification phase.

Step 6: This is called an 'anneal soak'. Keep the bung in to retain heat and to even out the kiln temperature. Each glass will have its own annealing point, and it is important to know what each one is. The kiln will cool to the annealing point of the glass being fired and hold there for a given time. This length of time will depend on the thickness of the glass, whether it has a mould around it or how complex the form is. The anneal soak allows everything to even out in temperature. The glass is returning to a solid state and this soaking enables all the molecules to even out in the glass, thus relieving strain. See the annealing section on p.115.

Step 7: This is the 'anneal cool to strain point'. Again keep the bung in to retain the heat. Each glass has its own strain point, information that is usually available from the manufacturer. The strain point is the lower point of the annealing zone, and it is important to cool slowly from the annealing point to the strain point, so as to relieve as much stress as possible in the glass.

Step 8: This final step is known as 'cooling to room temperature'. Once again, keep the bung in to retain the heat. After the strain point, all of the stress which can be removed should have been removed. This means it is possible to go a little faster down to room temperature. Once the kiln has reached 200°C (392°F), it can usually be turned off and left to drop naturally to room temperature before being opened. If you find yourself in a real rush and you need to reload the kiln as quickly as possible, the kiln can be opened at 100°C (212°F), and the work wrapped in newspaper and allowed to cool to room temperature undisturbed on a bench.

KILNS

There are many kilns readily available, suiting a wide range of glass techniques. Equally, there are a wide range of kilns designed specifically for fusing, slumping or casting. They can be very useful in making certain tasks easier and reducing potential problems. It is also worth noting that kilns do not have to be specifically designed for glassmaking.

I will outline the main considerations when selecting a kiln, and will examine some of the main advantages of the speciality kilns on the market.

Firstly, when looking at the main features of a kiln, there are three important factors to consider:
• loading and access;
• power requirements; and
• reading and controlling heat in the kiln.

Loading and access

An important consideration is the material that is going to be used in the kiln, and the technique used to form the glass. There are two main types of kiln on the market: top-loaders and front-loaders. Fusing kilns, which vary a little from these two, are covered on p.113. Both top- and front-loaders have pros and cons.

Top-loaders

These are quite often circular, with elements embedded all around the walls and in the lid, allowing even heat distribution. One drawback is that these kilns are often relatively tall narrow cylinders, so the heat tends to vary at different heights. This can be frustrating when you are trying to fire glass consistently. Top-loaders are economical both to buy and to run. As some will run with a three-pin plug and are on casters, they can literally be wheeled into, and used in, a studio. For certain techniques visual access can be restricted with a top-loader, which may make it difficult to monitor the firing process. Several shelves are stacked on top of each other during a firing, so only the top work will be visible when you open the lid. Also, rising heat makes it much harder to look into a top-loader when it is at the highest temperatures.

Front-loaders

These kilns come in a range of sizes. The heating elements can be distributed in a variety of ways, either down the sides, or around the two sides and the back, or covering the three internal walls with additional elements in the door. All of these arrangements have their advantages.

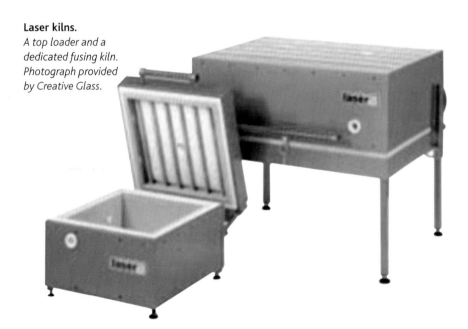

Laser kilns.
A top loader and a dedicated fusing kiln. Photograph provided by Creative Glass.

The one area it is best not to have elements is the floor. Any element coming into contact with hot molten glass will quickly be damaged and will need to be replaced. If liquid glass finds its way off the kiln shelves, it can easily fall onto the bottom of the kiln. This will take a lot of cleaning, before the kiln can be fired again. An element-free kiln floor allows you to spread a layer of plaster powder, or silica sand. This makes the removal of any glass overflow straightforward.

Another problem that can occur with front-loaders, namely cold spots, is dependent on how well the elements are distributed and how well the kiln is insulated. When inspecting a firing, or when crash-cooling, it is easy for the front of the kiln to get too cold while the door is open. This can cause potential cracking in the pieces. The advantage with a front-loading kiln is that all the shelves are visible when you are inspecting a firing. However, heat will still rise in front-loaders, as in top-loaders, which leads to a disparity between work at different levels in the kiln. The work at the top gets more heat, and fires at a higher temperature, than the work at the bottom.

Fusing kilns

As fusing projects tend to be flat, thin pieces, the kilns will echo this shape. They tend to have elements only in the top. They have wide flat bases with access from at least three sides on which to arrange a fusing project. The top of the kiln, including the elements, either levers up from the rear or is lowered down into position by pulleys when you need to fire up the kiln. The arrangement of elements in the top is a great advantage for fusing. The elements distribute the heat evenly from the top. The glass will melt evenly and the chances of a crack developing, as the kiln is heating up, are reduced. Thus the problem of side heat from top- and front-loaders has been eliminated. Cold spots, however, can be an issue. Crash-cooling has to be done with care, as the design of a fusing kiln, while assisting access, also allows air to rush in once the kiln lid is lifted.

Power requirements

The size of the kiln, and the number of elements it contains, will determine the heat output needed to obtain the necessary temperatures for the firings. This, in turn, will dictate the power input required from the electricity supply. Consideration must be given to the total available power input to the premises, where the kiln is to be located and what other equipment will be drawing on the electricity supply. This is a job for the professionals, so seek the advice of a qualified electrician before purchasing or installing a kiln, as they will be able to advise you on the specific limitations of your situation. This is not only a very important safety issue, which could see an overstretched electricity supply causing a fire; it could also mean ruined firings if incorrectly installed electrics lead to fuses blowing and kilns cutting out at crucial annealing points.

Reading and controlling heat in the kiln

For successful glass-firing is essential that you have an accurate reading of the temperature in the kiln, and also that you have a means of controlling it. This is done via a thermocouple inside the kiln linked to a controller with a digital readout for temperature and programming. Thermocouples are generally situated on the back wall towards the bottom of a front-loader, and towards the bottom of a top-loader. This may lead to a slightly lower temperature reading at the top of the kiln than is actually the case. Controllers are available with such a wide range of features that it is wise to discuss your particular needs with the manufacturers in order to find the most appropriate controller for you and the kiln. For glass, one of the most useful facilities is the option to heat up over several stages, hold at a given temperature and cool down over several stages. This tends to be beyond the ability of really basic controllers, but most middle-of-the-range ones may have the facility to link programs, which allows for much more flexibility. Controllers will require firing information in either set points or accumulated hours.

Once the information is put into the controller, it will quite simply switch the kiln on or off to attain certain temperatures in a given time. At certain points in the firing, it is useful to have the bung of the kiln either in or out, to help with heat control or to allow impurities to escape. I have detailed this information along with the firing curves for the individual projects at the end of this chapter. Each kiln will have its own peculiarities, and as you become familiar with them you will be able to adjust the firings accordingly.

ANNEALING

It is impossible to work with hot glass without having an understanding of the annealing process. If annealing is not carried out successfully, a piece will retain stress and, even if you are lucky enough to have it emerge from the kiln intact, it may crack or shatter at any moment. This could occur while you are cold-working or, disastrously, it has been known to happen weeks later in a gallery setting, taking many other pieces with it.

What is annealing? It is the slow cooling of glass in two stages from the anneal soak to the anneal cool. The annealing range has the annealing point at the top end and the strain point at the bottom. It varies from glass to glass and thus will be specific to any particular project. It is worth speaking with the supplier or manufacturer to work out what the annealing range will be for the glass and project you are working on.

Glass has a very long range of viscosity. Water goes from a liquid to a solid state when it freezes at the very specific temperature of 0°C (32°F). Metals behave in the same way when being heated for casting. The change from liquid to solid, or vice versa, is obvious. Glass does not give such convenient evidence of change. Glass moves slowly from solid to liquid and back again. Although these changes are not visually detectable, knowing the annealing point gives you warning of when the glass is moving from solid to liquid. This is useful information, as it means we can treat the glass in quite a different way if we are confident it is behaving like a liquid. For example, a more rapid heat can be applied, as a liquid cannot crack. Being able to anticipate when the glass is reaching this stage will help us to control devitrification (see the notes on devitrification on p.19). Equally, it is important to know the annealing point when the glass has been fired and is being cooled back to room

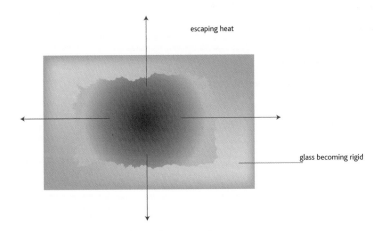

escaping heat

glass becoming rigid

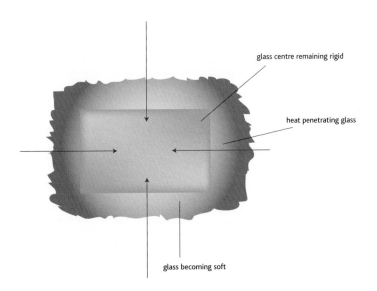

glass centre remaining rigid

heat penetrating glass

glass becoming soft

The heating and cooling of glass through the annealing point: When cooling, the outside of the glass begins to lose heat faster than the centre, which can lead to tension if it is not controlled. If the glass heats too quickly it can expand on the outside and crack if the centre is not given time to gain the same amount of heat. Diagram by Takako Tucker

temperature. If the glass falls below the hardening temperature too quickly, stress will occur and cracks may develop. To prevent this happening, slow controlled cooling is used. How does the slow cooling help to alleviate the stress in the glass? Glass is a very poor conductor of heat. As it cools, it will begin to shrink and harden. If this is done too quickly the outside of the glass will become rigid, while the middle of the glass, which is struggling to lose its heat, remains liquid. This results in the glass being compressed by the shrinking, cooling outer layer and so tension and cracks will occur. If the cooling or annealing is done correctly and slowly, the middle has a chance to lose equal amounts of heat, shrinking at the same rate as the outside, and so everything settles down nicely with any tension kept to a minimum. The kiln is held at the annealing point for a calculated length of time, the point at which we have determined the glass to be moving from a liquid to a solid state. This anneal soak allows all the residue heat struggling to escape from the middle of the glass, which is still above the annealing point, to dissipate before the anneal cool begins.

The annealing point is equally important when heating the glass. Just as with cooling, the glass does not conduct heat well. If too much heat is introduced to the glass too quickly when still below the annealing point, the outside will start to expand while the inside is still cool and rigid. This will cause stress and cracking (see opposite).

FIRINGS SCHEDULES AND CURVES

Fused brooch by Yoko Kuramoto

Glass used: hand-blown roundels made from Kugler colour
Kiln used: small front-loader

First firing: fusing-forming
370°C (698°F)/hour up to 760°C (1400°F)
Crash-cool down to 490°C (915°F)
48°C (119°F)/hour down to 250°C (482°F)
Turn the kiln off, then cool to room temperature.

Second firing: fire-polishing
325°C (616°F)/hour up to 650°C (1202°F)
Crash-cool down to 490°C (915°F)
48°C (119°F)/hour down to 250°C (482°F)
Turn the kiln off, then cool to room temperature.

Notes from the maker
These are very small pieces, so they go into a small kiln and don't require a lot of time to get up to top temperature. The mould for the fusing-firing is kept and reused for the fire-polishing firing.

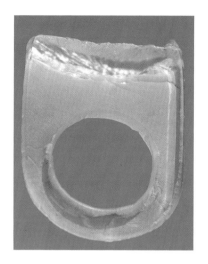

Plaster-fused ring by Yvonne Coffey

Glass used: 3 mm (0.1 in.) float
Kiln used: front-loader

Firing
100°C (212°F)/hour up to 850°C (1562°F), then soak for 30 minutes
Crash-cool down to 520°C (968°F)
50°C (122°F)/hour down to 320°C (608°F)
Turn the kiln off, then cool to room temperature.

Notes from the maker
The plaster tends to insulate the glass, so a lot of heat is required to ensure a good fuse is obtained. Float glass is quite hard and so will require more heat than a softer glass would need using this technique. This is a very small piece and does not have a lot of glass exposed, so the annealing is quite quick. The kiln used is very well insulated and cools down slowly.

Slumped necklace by Amanda Simmons

Glass used: 9 mm (0.35 in.) sheet Bullseye black glass fused with stringers
Kiln used: small fusing kiln with elements in the top only

Firing
95°C (203°F)/hour up to 720°C (1328°F) then soak for 20 minutes or until the glass has slumped sufficiently through the hole.
Crash-cool down to 540°C (1004°F) then soak for 20 minutes
Crash-cool down to 516°C (960°F) then soak for 30 minutes
30°C (86°F)/hour down to 371°C (700°F)
45°C (113°F)/hour down to room temperature

Notes from the maker
This sort of slumping will vary a lot depending on the thickness and type of glass. Just before the kiln reaches top temperature look inside to check how much it has moved; you are basically waiting for gravity to pull the glass down through the hole, making a perfect dome. When the glass has slumped to your requirements crash-cool the kiln to set the shape. This is the purpose of the first crash-cool, from 720° to 540°C (1328° to 1004°F).

Slumped necklace using ceramic-fibre paper by Debbi Collins

Glass used: thin salmon-pink Bullseye; and clear dichroic with a cover of clear Bullseye for the cabochon.
Kiln used: front loader

First firing
300°C (572°F)/hour up to 515°C (959°F)
Full heat up to 780°C (1436°F), no soak

Second firing for slump and fire-polishing
300°C (572°F)/hour up to 515°C (959°F)
Full heat up to 750°C (1382°F), no soak

Firing for the dichroic cabochon
300°C (572°F)/hour up to 515°C (959°F)
Full heat up to 800°C (1472°F), no soak

Notes from the maker
This is a slightly higher temperature than is normally used for a slumping, so that it both slumps and also rounds or bobbles up the ends of the armatures nicely all in one firing.

Cast ring by Angela Thwaites

Glass used: Banas
Kiln used: small front-loader

Firing
75°C (167°F)/ hour up to 200°C (392°F) then soak for 1 hour
100°C (212°F)/ hour up to 600°C (1112°F) then soak for 30 minutes
250°C (482°F)/ hour up to 840°C (1544°F) then soak for 1 hour
250°C (482°F)/ hour up to 850°C (1553°F) then soak for 30 minutes
250°C (482°F)/ hour down to 475°C (887°F) then soak for 3 hours
15°C (48°F)/ hour down to 350°C (662°F)
25°C (76°F)/ hour down to 150°C (302°F)
Turn the kiln off, then cool to room temperature.

Notes from the maker
The soaks at 200°C (392°F) and 600°C (1112°C) are to dry out the mould before the glass melts in. I think this gives a better final cast-glass surface and clarity. Once the mould is nice and dry, go up quickly, saving time and energy and hopefully avoiding the possibility of devitrification. The first top soak, at 840°C (1544°F), is so that the glass melts and goes into the mould at a lower temperature, saving the mould from being 'fried' and from cracking. The second top soak, at 850°C (1553°F), relaxes the glass into any details of fine texture and helps to bring up air bubbles as the glass is a bit more fluid.

Glossary

Bloom The dulling of the glass surface when affected by smoke or fumes.

Borosilicate glass Made from silicon and boric oxide. It has a low expansion rate and is used for kitchenware and scientific equipment.

Bullions Discs of glass.

Bung Removable kiln stopper.

Cast Melting glass into a mould.

Cerium oxide Used as a fine powder in the final stages of glass polishing.

Ceramic fibre paper Ceramic fibre insulation made into paperlike sheet and used for separating glass from moulds and kiln shelves.

China clay Highly refractory pure clay made from decomposed granite.

Coefficient of expansion A measurement of the amount by which a material expands when exposed to heat.

Cork wheel Used with a pumice to polish glass.

Crystal lead glass A brilliant clear glass with at least 30% lead oxide.

Dell de Vere Slabs of glass.

Dichroic glass Glass which has been chemically treated to transmit two different colours of light.

Devitrification The formation of crystals on glass.

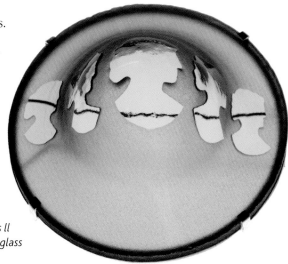

Cameo portrait brooch from series ll by Tarja Lahtinen. Recycled bottle glass sandblasted and set in silver.

Spring Thing brooch by Annette Paskiewicz. Laser-cut glass set in silver

Felt wheel Used with cerium for the final polishing of glass.

Firing cycle The process of heating and cooling the kiln.

Fire polishing Heating the glass in the kiln to give it a shine.

Flashed glass Glass with a fine layer of colour over it.

Flexi-drive A suspended motor with a flexible shaft leading to a hand piece which will take a variety of burrs.

Flint Mixed with plaster for the making of refractory moulds.

Float glass Sheet glass made by floating molten glass on a bed of molten tin.

Frit Glass granules.

Fusing Glass heated in the kiln to form a permanent bond.

Grinding Forming and shaping glass using abrasives.

Hard glass Glass that requires more heat to melt it.

Hand-lapping Grinding the glass by hand using various grades of carborundum powder.

Investment materials Used to make moulds for casting glass.

Kiln Insulated oven with elements used to heat glass for a variety of techniques.

Lost wax A wax model is encased in a refractory mould, the wax is melted out and the glass is melted into the cavity.

Mohs scale of hardness A scale devised by Friedrich Mohs to compare the relative hardness of a mineral.

Polishing Creating a shine via the kiln, abrasives or acid.

Pumice Volcanic rock ground to various grades.

Pyrex Borosilicate glass with very little expansion.

Quartz Mineral silica used in refractory moulds.

Rondels Circular discs of blown glass.

Soak Holding the kiln at a specific temperature.

Slumping Heating glass in the kiln until it bends.

Striking Colour or opacity altered when the glass is heated in a kiln.

Soft glass Glass which requires less heat to melt it.

Thermocouples Relay the temperature in the kiln back to the controller.

Viscosity The fluidity of molten glass.

Vitrification Materials turning into glass.

Suppliers

Bohle UK Ltd
Tameside Industrial Park
5th Avenue, Dukinfield
Cheshire SK16 4PP
Tel: 0044 (0)161 342 1100
www.bohle.ltd.uk
Glass-cutting tools, glass-bonding glue, tools, fittings.

Cottrell & Co.
Kingsway West
Dundee DD2 3QD
Tel: 0800 668 899
www.wright-cottrell.co.uk
Dental supplies, diamond burrs, thin sheet wax.

Creative Glass
Unit 12 Sextant Park, Neptune Close,
Medway City Estate
Rochester, Kent ME2 4LU
Tel: 0044 (0)1634 735416
www.creative-glass.com
Fusing glass, casting glass, tools, kilns, books.

D.K. Holdings
Station Approach, Staplehurst
Kent TN12 0QN
Tel: 0044 (0)1580 891 662
www.dk.holdings.co.uk
Grinding & drilling equipment; diamond pads, files & burrs.

Fairfield Displays
127 Albert Street, Fleet
Hampshire GU51 3SN
Tel: 01252 812211
www.fairfielddisplays.co.uk
Display equipment

H.S. Walsh & Sons Ltd
243 Beckenham Road, Beckenham
Kent BR3 4TS
Tel: 0044 (0)20 8778 7061
www.hswalsh.com
Jewellery tools, pumice, cerium, books.

Pearson's Glass
Unit 9, Lyon Way, Greenford
Middlesex UB6 0BN
Tel: 0044 (0)208 578 5788
www.pearsonsglass.com
Fusing and casting glass, tools, kilns, books.

Poth Hill & Co Ltd
Tel: 0044 (0)1708 526 828
www.poth-hill.co.uk
Microcrystalline wax and other specialist waxes.

P.V.S(UK)Ltd
Tel: 01274616941
www.pvsuk.com
Dedicated glass fusing supplier

Temsford Stained Glass
21 Church Street, Tempsford,
Sandy, Beds SG19 2AW
Tel: 0044 (0)1767 640 235
www.tempsfordstainedglass.co.uk
Kilns, fusing supplies, grinders, ring saws, cutters.

Alec Tiranti Ltd
3 Pipers Court, Berkshire Drive,
Thatcham, Berks RG19 4ER
Tel: 0044 (0)845 123 2100
www.tiranti.co.uk
Wax modelling materials, tools, Gelflex, books.

Bibliography

27fishes, *Wearing Glass: Contemporary Jewellery and Body Adornment* (27fishes, 2005), ISBN 0-9551372-0-9.

Beaver, Philippa, Domenech, Ignasi & Pascual, Eva, *Warm Glass: A Complete Guide to Kiln-forming Techniques* (Lark Books, 2005), ISBN 84-342-2554-9.

Bray, Charles, *Dictionary of Glass: Materials and Techniques* (London: A&C Black, 1995), ISBN 0 7136 4008 1.

Colclough, John, *Mould Making* (London: A&C Black, 1999), ISBN 1-889250-15-5.

Cummings, Keith, *Techniques of Kiln-formed Glass* (London: A&C Black, 1997), ISBN 0 7136 5342 6.

Fraser, Simon, *Contemporary Japanese Jewellery* (London: Merrell Publishers Ltd, 2001), ISBN 1-85894-163-6.

Halem, Henry, *Glass Notes: A Reference for the Glass Artist* (Franklin Mills Press, 1996), ISBN 1-885663-02-1.

Holzach, Cornelia, Ilse-Newman, Ursula & Page, Jutta-Annette, *GlassWear: Glass in Contemporary Jewellery* (Stuttgart: Arnoldsche, 2007), ISBN 978-3-89790-274-9.

McCreight, Tim, *The Complete Metalsmith,* (Davis Publications, Inc., 1991), ISBN 0-87192-240-1.

McCreight, Tim, *Jewellery: Fundamentals of Metalsmithing* (London: A&C Black, 1997), ISBN 0-7136-4900-3.

Mitsushima, Kazuko, *Glass Jewellery* (Bee Books, 2003), ISBN 4-89615-888-1.

Walker, Brad, *Contemporary Warm Glass* (Four Corners International, Inc., 2004), ISBN 0-97009334-9.

Index